Developing
Your "People Potential":
Key to Success in
Supervisory Management

Developing
Your "People Potential":
Key to Success in
Supervisory Management

King MacRury

Parker Publishing Company, Inc.
West Nyack, New York

Library of Congress Cataloging in Publication Data

MacRury, King
    Developing your "people potential."

    Bibliography: p.
    1. Supervision of employees. I. Title.
HF5549.M286   658.3'02   74-7318
ISBN 0-13-205484-1

Printed in the United States of America

To Beth — who taught me that when you place justifiable confidence in the people you work with, you build their confidence in themselves — and in you.

HOW THIS BOOK WILL HELP YOU

As a result of reading this book, you should:

— See yourself more clearly, accurately, and objectively, "as others see you" — and thus discover *how* and *why* they respond.
— Understand what your workers expect of you — and *what, how, why,* and *how much* you should fulfill this expectancy.
— Find suggestions for the most appropriate and effective means for placing values on jobs — and getting full value from your people.
— Discover new means of sincerely utilizing your own personality and interest to better your communications and relationships, make them more productive and rewarding.
— Find that it will not only help you to discover what you can do to progress more surely and quickly — but also will assist you in deciding *whether or not* "vertical" promotion is what you really want, are suited for, and should seek.

No matter what your supervisory management interest or responsibility is, there are 18 specific and fundamental ways in which this book will help you increase the effectiveness and motivational impact of your supervision, guidance, and leadership of people, will help you meet new and more extreme standards and requirements, and will help you improve personally and professionally in the satisfaction you receive from your work and your human relationships.

1. This book will help you to attain more reasonable and well-founded confidence in your acquired knowledge and your capacity to get the job done.
2. This book will help in your decision-making. There is no source for answers and formulas, but the support and affirmation you need are in the experiences and observations of other supervisors — the experiences you will find discussed in this volume.
3. This book will specifically help you to determine what you need to know about people in order to understand them, and how to effectively and accurately secure this information.

4. You will find many ideas and experiences of managers like your-self in this book. As you know, the information your fellow managers provide can be an invaluable and unlimited resource. Other sources are referred to and guidance is given on how they can best be studied, understood and applied.

5. This book will help you to see yourself and your supervisory position in a new light, and in the perspective of what is expected of you; thus it will help you to know *when* and *how* to apply your experience and knowledge for your greatest benefit.

6. It will give you a chance to compare with experienced colleagues many of your experiences, conclusions, and decisions — many of which you may previously have privately questioned.

From my observation of supervisory managers and their development, I believe you demand more from your reading — and you get it. If you are going to be tempted into giving your time and effort to reading, it must be about things which you can utilize.

For these reasons, this book is grounded on actual, practical, day-to-day experiences, all by and with supervisory managers: where theories and developments are outlined and recommended, they are always directly and clearly related to cases you will recognize and relate to your own personal and professional experiences.

The supervisory managers and executives from whose experiences and observations this book is composed are from virtually every type of industry and business enterprise, from every region of the United States and Canada, from a number of Asian and Pacific countries; also used as source material are the comments of supervisory managers and executives visiting in this country from at least twenty additional nations. In effect, the book both emphasizes the value of practical supervisory management experience and observations, and reflects their similarity and "exchange value," no matter where they may take place.

                                                        King MacRury

TABLE OF CONTENTS

1

HOW TO FIND AND MEASURE
YOUR "PEOPLE POTENTIAL"

It now takes a lesser number of *minutes* for a cosmonaut to circle the globe than it took days for Magellan to make his historic voyage: the meaning of *time* and *speed* has changed. A huge missile is targeted on a millions-of-miles-distant planet with infinitely greater precision than that' with which marksman Daniel Boone shot his bears from a few feet away: the meaning of *accuracy* has changed.

These are the qualities and capacities of products which industry has produced. To accomplish this, industry necessarily has had to change and update. Within industry, too, equally dramatic alteration has taken place. For instance, one worker and his machine may now produce more than the total output of a hundred to a thousand millhands of a few years past. Thus, the meaning of *volume* and of human capacity also has changed.

And the man in the middle of all that is changing in industry is the supervisory manager, who often is now responsible for more daily production than the total quota of an entire plant in 1920. The supervisory manager is no longer just the guy hired to stand around and see that the workers are doing what they have been instructed to do. Nor is he just the super-technician who merely matches up the physical motions of people with the technical demands of the machinery. The present-day supervisory manager is a thinker, planner, translator, and guide. To an extent unthinkable a few years ago, the supervisory manager is responsible for transforming theories into tangibles, plans into products.

His job has changed; his circumstances have changed; his work load, objectives and materials have changed. But the most vital and dramatic change of all is in people themselves. And in these changes especially, the supervisor-manager, who is the "human linkage" of the company, is truly in the middle of things. He must understand, promote, implement, and adapt to management changes, to mechanical and technological changes, to changes in his job itself. He must himself understand change so well that he can transmit this understanding to his work people, and prepare their attitudes, skills, responses, and assignments. In effect, he must change workers themselves, as necessary. Simultaneously, he must understand and productively cope with changes which are taking place in his people themselves. He must understand and cope with their changing ideas, concepts, attitudes, and values, as well as their responses, adaptation, and adjustment toward the change for which he is operationally responsible.

It has been suggested that "change *is* people." Change most assuredly affects people, is influenced by people, is accomplished by people, is a product of people. To the extent that change affects, involves, or influences his people, related responsibility is almost totally centered in a supervisor-manager.

Skill and Performance Requirements Are Changing

Some people find it particularly difficult to learn new methods and to adjust to changes. "That's one reason I've liked my job so much," paper-sorter Margaret MacLeod told me. "In the 40 years I've been on this job, there probably have been fewer changes in it than in any other job in the plant; changes in my job have been so gradual that I haven't had too much trouble keeping up with it. But all jobs have changed — and sometimes it's a little startling when I think of all the things that are different in methods and the machinery and equipment that are new even in my job; you've got to know quite a bit more about equipment than was true when I started out."

When we think of changing occupations, we are more inclined to think about manual labor jobs which have been eliminated and the machine-related occupations which have replaced them. Or we tend to think about the new occupations and technologies which have sprung up in connection with certain specific new equipment — technologies such as computerization, mechanization, and automation — which to most of us are symbols of industrial change. But this is misleading: change does not pertain solely to manual jobs and occupations. In a seminar which I was conducting on the West Coast, technological supervisors raised the question, "What do you do with a 56-year-old vacuum tube engineer?" And, in reality, engineering — which is the resource from which changed technology has come — is itself more subject to change and obsolescence than any other area or occupation.

And when you start thinking about change, don't confine your thoughts to your need to view new ideas and equipment (and quotas) flexibly and receptively. Also, don't restrict your thoughts to the problems of obsolescence in the skills and equipment of your department — and to your need to adjust and cope. Because to effectively perform your responsibilities relating to change, you must foresee the potential for change and its probable nature. You must, insofar as possible, prepare your people and your department in advance. To the greatest possible extent, you must convert your people and their skills to new requirements. In so doing, you reduce the problems of transition and the impact of obsolescence, loss, and layoff.

We can summarize this responsibility into eight specific activities which you must adopt:

1. Determine accurately the specific current needs of each occupation under your jurisdiction.
2. Ascertain the degree to which actual needs are met by current skills of workers assigned to your department.
3. Calculate what additional current and immediate future needs of the department can be met by personnel training and development, and which must be fulfilled from recruiting outside the department or company.
4. Maintain alert awareness of the changes which are taking place in the company, in operational methods, in occupations, and in the equipment and materials which influence occupational methods and contents.
5. Relate and communicate in-process and anticipated alteration of skill needs and requirements, as reflected by changes denoted in the company and in the processes pertaining to your department's operation.
6. Translate current and pending changes of operations and operating methods into work assignments, occupations, and skill specifications.
7. Determine how future skill and personnel requirements relate to the potentialities and capacities of department employees — and

how they will obsolete, replace, or terminate current assignments.
8. Provide guidance, stimulation, training, and assistance to workers whose skills must be altered, transformed, or replaced.

Unfortunate and Unworkable Alternatives

It becomes pretty obvious that both preparing for change, and adjusting to it with maximum effectiveness and minimum loss and disruption, require a great deal of sensitive direct attention. And only a supervisor-manager has the combined knowledge of and sensitivity to the needs of individual occupations and the potentialities of individual workers to fulfill these requirements. Without such direct attention, several problems arise. The alternative to such direct consideration by an immediate supervisor is more remote review and decision, conducted by a centralized department, as part of the company strategy.

No centralized department can ever attain the sensitive, detailed understanding that an effective supervisor has of each employee. And no centralized department can ever be so minutely familiar with individual occupations as to know their capacity for adjustment to change. Problems of occupations and of people must necessarily be generalized to an unfortunate extent when handled independently by a centralized company department.

In the earlier years of our current pace of change and progress — before the recent recession — we learned a number of lessons which we should not ever forget. Industry's primary emphasis at that time was on technology — and the securing of people who were skilled in the newest technologies. The role of supervisory managers in planning, selecting, defining, and assigning of technological talents was minimized. Manpower planning, recruitment, and assignment were centralized. Without the support of the supervisory managers' knowledge of appropriate occupations and the production and output propensities of individual people, the numbers as well as the range of specific talents were not sufficiently clear. Centralized planning thus led to recruitment handled primarily from outside the company, inadequate attention was given to potentialities of the people currently employed, and there was "feather bedding" in both the numbers of technical people and the variety of technical skills. Because without knowledge of individual people and occupations, it becomes impossible to foresee how much of the future need can be met by retraining, adjustment, reassignment.

When handled on a centralized basis, the major issue becomes one of assuring the availability of suitable talents and qualifications, when and as required. Without precise and dependable analysis of what current and future skill requirements consist of, the centralized planner has a strong tendency to over-provide for unforeseen eventualities by hiring excessive numbers of excessively qualified people. One company, for instance, was accused of hiring ten engineers of varied specializations in anticipation of an ill-defined problem which management believed might arise within the next year. It was believed that the company would thus be employing someone of the engineering specialization it would ultimately require, and that the nine who were thereby not specifically needed would be laid off.

Although recession and the need for more proficient and economic staffing have eliminated a tendency toward feather bedding, some of the results of these practices are well worth remembering. In the first place, the problems created at the time clearly demonstrated the vital importance of supervisors' skills and knowledge in placing and motivating people. And furthermore, in the effort to reduce the extreme costs and impact of the "shotgun" method of hiring, to make maximum use of the personnel they hired companies assigned these workers at one, two, or three levels below their levels of qualification. This practice proved destructive among both newly hired specialists and other employees as well. For example, engineers assigned to work at technician levels became demoralized — and the technicians whose responsibilities they took over became demoralized, feeling that their prospects for progress and development had thereby been eliminated.

There is no substitute for the knowledge of supervisory managers in personnel planning — and their participation and involvement in it.

What Happens When Specifications Don't Fit the Actual Work

The effect of inaccurate job descriptions — which lead to inadequacy of skills required by departmental operations — is pretty obvious: at best, it means the scramble, hiring "from the outside," disruption to the work force and its morale; at worst, it means that the department's work just doesn't get done. But when inaccurate job descriptions sin on the side of developing or securing *over-*

qualified people, the problems thereby created are at least equally basic and important.

A young engineer attending a mid-west seminar complained, "I was hired a year-and-a-half in advance of my graduation. I was selected because my interests and qualifications seemed to fit precisely the hiring specifications and job description of my company. But I have been with my company for almost two years — and I haven't yet been assigned to one of the 36 activities which were listed in the hiring and job specifications. I can tell you this: I'm demoralized."

Probably by the time this young man was assigned to the work for which he was qualified — if, indeed, that time ever came — he would have left the company, or become diminished in his skill or demoralized in his attitudes to the point at which his qualifications would be relatively worthless.

There is nothing more stimulating to people than a sense of accomplishment and progress. And there is nothing more debilitating than to be depreciated in their capabilities, or contributions.

An experienced and observant supervisory manager ultimately becomes extremely impressed with the tremendous capacity of people to learn, develop capability and to progress. In so doing, he learns the meaning of his own "people potential." He learns that, in being assigned as a supervisor, his own capacity is determined by the capability and sensitivity with which he sees, inspires, guides, and applies this tremendous capacity which is latent in people. In effect, his capacity is the aggregate capacity of all of his work people. His success and accomplishment are in the extent to which he discovers, recognizes, develops, and activates the capabilities of his people. The more he understands people, the more he appreciates and attains his "people potential."

Jobs are changing — and work situations and requirements are changing. The problems of assignment are complex, and are made all the more difficult by the rapid changes which are taking place in technology, industries, society, people and work relationships. But the challenging and rewarding job of developing, assigning, utilizing, and motivating people is largely centered in your responsibilities as supervisory manager. You can commence the fulfillment of these responsibilities by:

- Knowing the job: outline and describe it completely and accurately; communicate its requirements clearly, comprehensively, understandably.

- Knowing the worker: fully utilize his skills and motivated efforts.
- Knowing the prospect of change: understand and project its effects on the department, and prepare your people's skill and understanding.
- Knowing your people's potentialities: guide them in development, preparation, and progress.

Getting Your "People Potential" to Help in Implementing Changes

Bill Whelan is a computer supervisor. When offered his current job with an old line New England company, Bill was warned in advance that the previous computer supervisor had been defeated and had resigned because of employee resistance and their refusal to cooperate.

Bill had carefully studied the background of the company and had found that its productivity far exceeded that of competitive firms which were utilizing similar traditional operating practices. He commented, "I have a great deal of respect for these people — they had accomplished more than anyone else who was working with similar methods, equipment, techniques. It made me think of the tremendous potential they would have, if they applied this same capacity to more productive means and equipment."

It soon became apparent that Bill's predecessor had been so exclusively concerned with the equipment he supervised that he approached the whole problem in terms of the potentiality of his machinery, giving no thought to the potentiality of people. Bill approached this in an opposite direction. He said to people, "You have been doing a fantastic job; but the present-day demands of industry are just too great and too intense. If we can make this equipment useful to you — make it work for you — I believe that with the capacity you folks have demonstrated, we'll soon be far ahead of the entire industry!"

Because he was unfamiliar with the industry, Bill learned about it from the "old hands." He studied and determined precisely what was essential, "what the job consists of." Then he carefully developed a program which tied in the computer capacities to the specific major problems of the operation. "Regardless of the extreme respect I had at the very beginning for the capacities and potentialities of these people, the old timers still surprise me," he commented. "In addition to helping me with my questions, they came to me with suggestions which made it possible for me to apply the computer to a multitude of areas that I would never have thought of. This computer system may be helping them to realize their potential a little more fully and profitably — but their response demonstrated a measure of their personal potential which I don't think you realized they had to offer."

Taking a Critical Look at Your Job Specifications and Work Demands

When we recognize that all jobs everywhere are changing, and changing rapidly, we are somewhat prepared for the gradual evolutionary differences that creep unnoticed into the operations and the conduct of all jobs. Ten years ago, in discussing recruiting programs, I used to suggest that if job specifications had not been reviewed in two or three years, they should be carefully evaluated for possible changes before being used as the basis for recruiting new people. Now I suggest that this be done every six months — and if there is no turnover in a specific occupation, that its description be reviewed and analyzed at least annually.

Nevertheless — despite planned periodic reviews — some supervisory managers are often quite startled to find how many changes creep in unnoticed. Occasionally I work with clients in developing job evaluation programs. Part of the technique of job evaluation is to have each individual fill in a job-description questionnaire, covering his own occupation. The purpose of this is to assure that the final descriptions are accurate and comprehensive. Also, because these questionnaires are reviewed by the direct supervisors of the people involved, the technique highlights and helps to resolve any differences in opinion between the supervisor and the job incumbent as to what the occupation actually consists of. In recent years I have heard many supervisors comment, after discussing completed questionnaires with the employees who filled them in, "Gee — there are a number of things that have sneaked in — a number of changes which have taken place in the job about which I was not fully aware."

Descriptions — and related deployment of work loads — should be reviewed annually, or prior to:

1. any new recruiting;
2. any reassignment or shift in department personnel;
3. any projection or estimate of future potentialities for individuals or groups of workers;

4. the formulation of training or development programs;
5. annual review and appraisal of workers' performance;
6. counsel of individual employees regarding their need for development in skills training;
7. introduction or installation of any major equipment or machinery, or procedure or method change in the department;
8. major changes in the company organization, structure, or operation;
9. turnover or other personnel alterations of the department; or
10. after change in supervisory management of department.

The Revision of Job Content

Bear in mind that the decisions you reach in reviewing job content and requirements may have a fundamental effect on the career development of your department's workers. It may also have a strong impact on the department's capacity to produce and to meet its quotas. So your review must be comprehensive, and it must be accurate. Whenever questions occur, you must allow time for adequate exploration. You may find it necessary or helpful to consult one or more of the workers assigned to the occupations in question. As a matter of fact, discussion with individual workers may assist you in strengthening mutual understanding and recognition of job content and requirements as well as reinforcing the accuracy of the job review.

Every major change in the equipment or operating method is accompanied by a variety of alterations in procedure. Such procedural or methods changes assist in your occupational review. Your approach then becomes largely a matter of tracing procedural changes through the occupations to which they apply, noting revisions and deletions made necessary by the procedural changes. However, when this device is used, you should remember that alterations in occupational content may also be caused by procedures which do not in themselves apply to the specific occupation. Also, major alterations in the procedures of departments adjacent or interrelated to yours may affect the content of some of your deparment's own occupations, even though you may not be directly involved in the procedure which is being changed.

For instance, a procedural change which alters the number of employees in an adjacent department — or its output — necessarily will affect your department. This is especially true if any of your occupations relate to the other department in work flow.

In other words, known changes which have taken place in procedures can highlight the need to reexamine occupational content.

But you cannot safely restrict your review of occupations to those which are directly involved in the procedures which have been changed.

What Job Changes to Look For

As you reexamine job contents and descriptions, critically ask yourself how many of the requirements . . .

- a) are needed, appropriate, apply;
- b) are unnecessary;
- c) are suited to previous activity, and are in need of updating or replacement;
- d) are obsolete; and
- e) are redundant and ridiculous.

These may seem like strong and caustic criticisms, but they apply in more cases than most of us readily admit.

Al Romano, in taking over as superintendent of a box board plant, had issued instructions that a certain kind of filler was to be used in the make. A month or so later, as he stood watching the operation, he noticed that his instructions were being followed: the brand of filler he preferred was being used — but so were four other brands. When he questioned the workmen, he discovered that his predecessors also had had a preference for other brands. As he had done, previous superintendents had merely given orders, and had never explained them. The workers had no idea as to what they were adding — or why. So, because prior orders had not been rescinded when they were instructed to use new brands, they merely added these materials to those which they had previously utilized.

In my professional activity, so many similar cases are found that it becomes a little amusing. I recall, for example, noting that one particular operating report was being prepared in twelve different ways. When questioned, the controller reflected that eight of the twelve were ways devised by prior executives — one by a president who had been dead for nearly 25 years: he had never been able to secure authorization for discontinuing the obsoleted reports. Yet the fact that they were prepared each month had considerable influence on the requirements and skills, the work load, and the number of people in his department.

Many, many institutions, companies, offices, plants, and departments are similarly haunted by ghosts of prior managers.

As is suggested later in this volume in regard to discipline, unless work demands are supported by reason, appropriateness, and usefulness, the attitude and morale of work people will be seriously affected. Failure to explain not only adds to the burden of unnecessary work-effort and wasted skill; it also raises the question in the minds of your subordinates as to your knowledge and accuracy in establishing assignments, activities, and work requirements.

Workers' Qualifications Must Be Fully Utilized

Economic recession reduced the tendency toward the feather bedding mentioned earlier. And the reduction was in both ways: first it was in the previous effort to hire excessive numbers of qualified people; and second in the penchant which some concerns had for hiring people whose qualifications and price tags exceeded actual minimum requirements.

But apart from the price tag and other economic issues, it is vitally important that you hire people who *meet* and do not *exceed* the necessary qualifications for work. For instance, we know that favorable morale and motivation are attained only when people find a sense of self-worth in their work, when they feel that their skills are needed — and that there is prospect for growth.

Even when qualification requirements are precisely accurate and jobs are staffed with people ideally suited in talents, interests, and capabilities, a major supervisory responsibility still remains to be solved. A company staffed with the most qualified and precisely suited personnel could quickly become bankrupt. Employee qualifications are the frozen assets of the corporation, until they are activated, assigned, directed, and motivated. And this "unfreezing" process is exclusively the responsibility of supervisory managers.

Orienting and Fitting People into Work

You have first assured the *need* for the qualifications represented by the people you have hired into the department — and those in the department to whom you have provided guidance in training and development. You have, second, made certain that your people are oriented to the overall needs of the department, and to the specific requirements of the occupations to which they are assigned. It is next necessary to ensure that people are utilized to the fullest degree of their competence and capability.

There are brief periods, at the outset of new or changed assignments, when you obviously cannot expect to receive the full benefits of employees' qualifications. So you make advanced provision for this. Training or learning periods, probation, and orientation, all are extremely helpful. These are periods during which new employees' activities are kept under fairly close surveillance, and are restricted to more routine and controllable job responsibilities.

But such break-in programs must be carefully planned and explained in advance. The restrictions, limitations, and close surveillance should not be continued beyond the originally stipulated time without conference with each employee who is involved. Before the original program is altered, there should be development of mutual understanding and agreement on the reason for protracting the program.

Rather than protracting these orientation programs, supervisory managers are often inclined to assume that they will accomplish their desired purpose in the originally established time schedule. In other words, orientation and probationary periods are merely explained to workers; employees are then left to their own devices unless they themselves raise questions. And on the termination of the agreed time, workers are catapulted into full responsibility, without any additional communications or guidance.

New Assignment Is a Mutual Learning Period

The early days of assignment to a job should be a learning experience for the supervisor-manager as well as for the worker. New to the job — regardless of comparable prior experience — the worker should have a number of questions. Many of these questions will pertain to his own need to learn and understand. However, experienced supervisors have learned that the nature of questions very often reveals the need for changes in occupation content or method, and often yields suggestions for improvement and expediting of work loads and work assignment.

It is, as many supervisors have termed it, "a fresh look at the job and the work load." One supervisor-manager remarked, "The kind of questions I received from newly assigned workers made me suddenly realize that I was expecting people to do things as I would do them, when, perhaps, their own approaches would have been equally satisfactory and would have yielded equally effective results." The fact is, that by giving workers latitude to exercise their own initiative, a supervisory manager does much to increase and intensify their motivation.

Much can additionally be learned and understood about the worker himself from the way he approaches new activity, the kinds of questions he asks, his efforts, his relations with other people, and his attitudes and interest.

1. Does he ask questions?
2. Are his questions clear and pertinent?
3. Do his questions reflect effort to understand — or to debate instructions?
4. Do his questions reflect thought about constructive and improved approaches?
5. Does he proceed with partial understanding, and try to work things out for himself?
6. How does he respond to suggestions and corrections?
7. Does he ask questions of other workers?
8. Does he appear to try to extend cooperation to others?
9. What kind of responsiveness does he appear to inspire in other workers?
10. Does he ask questions about the place and relationship of his work to other occupations, people, and processes?

Suitability Changes, Too

For years, "turnover" has been regarded as a dirty word in employee relations. I'd like to suggest that turnover is undesirable only when it indicates or results from some specifically negative problem of administration and worker relations. Of course it is negative in the sense of being an intense scheduling problem when it is unannounced, erratic, unplanned, unpredictable. And the fact that it *is* erratic and unannounced usually reveals a bad situation of communications and morale.

Some operations would specifically benefit from turnover. For instance, in some assembly work it has been found that after an initial training period productivity and quality continue to climb slowly for a period of three years. Thereafter, they level off and remain on a virtual plateau for about a year and a half. Then they start to diminish — and never again reach the peak. Transfer, promotion, retraining, occupational change, or turnover obviously would be useful.

As another example of occupational circumstances in which transfer or turnover might be mutually useful, accident proneness seems to increase on some jobs when people have been assigned for long periods. Yet there appears to be no age-and-accident correlation. One such occupation is that of the papermill supercalendar operator. Newly assigned personnel usually do not work directly enough with the machinery to be exposed to hazard. In the earlier years of actual operation of equipment, the accident record usually is favorable, but some plants have found that almost all accidents are incurred by people who have operated the equipment for ten years or longer.

But turnover also may be strategically built in for the mutual benefit of the employee and the company. Small concerns, which have definite limits in promotional prospects yet which feel the need for the services of ambitious young men and women, do well to attract and employ such people and mutually and candidly plan for relatively short tenure. Such firms in effect substitute educational benefits for growth-and-progress possibilities. And since promotion prospects are not available within the company, training and education are offered which ultimately over-qualify the young workers for job opportunities within the company. This provides them the asset of development which they thereafter can apply to work with a new employer, a company which is larger, and in which such promotion possibilities *do* exist.

Mutual Benefit in Turnover

One company which has adopted such a plan of strategically planned turnover is versatile and is in such an intensively competitive industry that wages and salary rates are relatively low. Screening procedures are extremely sensitive and selective. Excellent support is given to education and training programs. Morale is high, and turnover is carefully planned, foreseen, and compensated.

Another firm which operates with planned turnover is somewhat larger — an "old line" company. The central problem in this company was that it had operated with traditional methods and products for such a long period that its predominantly long-service and aging employees presented a serious obstacle as the firm was suddenly confronted with the need for extensive changes and updating. Economically unable to undertake the extensive early retirement program which would have been necessary, the company adopted a plan for employment and training of zealous young people whose interest, management realized, would endure only for the period of their training, development, and education. The fact that some occupations were dead-end because of the lack of higher-level jobs requiring the same nature of skill, or because they were already occupied by immobilized or non-promotable senior people, thus did nothing to dampen the enthusiasm and the prospects of the ambitious young people.

A key supervisor-manager commented, "We can expect about three to four years' service from these young people — and during that period we invest heavily in their training, development, and education. But during that period, we get their ideas, interests, motivated effort. Their contribution is four to five times that of our long-term people — and we part as friends. What we plan to add to our program in the future is some form of assistance to help these young people get jobs with other companies, once they have completed their training and have exhausted all the progress we can offer."

Vocational Guidance — and Assistance

Still another firm — a somewhat larger one, but one in which only relatively low or medium skill levels were required — went one step further. Study was made of the larger and faster-growing concerns in the area. Lists were made of occupations in larger companies for which young people might suitably prepare themselves while working for the firm.

Working on a cooperative basis with these other local concerns and with educational institutions in the area, the firm established an integrated development program which included, also, their own in-company training facilities. Growth and future prospects thus could be made reasonably clear to ambitious young people and appropriate guidelines could be used in suggesting specific courses and directions of educational development.

It is interesting to note that in each of these cases supervisory managers played a key and predominant part. It was their suggestions and recommendations that initiated the programs. And, apart from administrative assistance in outside contact activity and in personnel records, the specific courses and directions, worker-selections, and governing policy, all were formulated by supervisory managers from analyses of their own departmental needs and interests, and those of their workers.

It is also interesting to note the degree to which this reflected supervisory managers' ability to see their workers' potentialities. These supervisors obviously had developed the capacity to under-

stand the specific needs of their departments and occupations —
and to recognize suitable potentialities in their work people. These
supervisory managers actually were able to identify the potentialities of their workers beyond the needs of their departments and
occupations.

Ways of Figuring Up Your Subordinates' Potentialities Accurately

Unfortunately we are often misled and inhibited, or "hung up,"
by paying too close attention to a worker's previous experience or
stated interests. Who is to say, really, that a worker has not been
misguided in his initial selection of an occupation? That he may not
have taken a specific kind of job because of temporary financial
necessity? Or accepted a certain job because he was "sold a bill of
goods"? Or that he undertook it because he believed that it would
assist him to attain certain career objectives or status which he had
selected for himself?

The very first step in assessing the potentiality of people is to
ignore all previous experience. The second is to equally ignore all
of the well-clarified statements of a worker's aims and objectives.
These are *later* considerations — and should not be allowed to mislead or inhibit initial analyses. Experience is a "vested interest" of
the worker and is a value insofar as the department and pending
assignment are concerned, but it must be evaluated in terms of how
it can be best applied in relation to the worker's basic potentialities.

Similarly, preconceived aims and objectives must be related to
the actualities of the worker's potentialities and development capacities; sometimes these need amendment, sometimes they can be
strengthened by specific guidelines as to how they can be achieved,
by what means, and when. After all, aims and objectives are merely
the "energizers" by which human effort is stimulated toward the
fulfillment of a worker's potentialities.

Bear in mind that, within the limits of normalcy, people can do
anything: there probably is no person on earth who cannot do more
and develop more capability than he realizes. One of the most fascinating and rewarding aspects of the job of supervisory management is that it places a man or a woman in a position to *see* this in
people, to *develop* it in people — and to surprise people themselves
by the extent of their own potentialities.

A Key: How Do Jobs and Qualifications Meet People's Interests

Our first step, therefore, is to select and define the specific things, occupations, and activities in which the individual's potentialities are greatest, have greatest support, and are most likely to develop. These are evident in a worker's interests: interests reveal both the nature of the activities in which a worker will be most responsive, and the specific kinds of things the individual must exercise and satisfy — either occupation or in non-occupational activity, or in a combination of the two — in order to achieve a sense of self-value and well-being.

This review also should be uninhibited, and should not be influenced by previous work record, experience, or occupational considerations. Whether done by interview, discussion, observation, analysis of prior personal tendencies and work records, by psychological testing, or — most dependably — by a combination of all of them, the entire range of interests should be carefully explored.

For instance, how do such interests as the following compare in relative intensity — and which are positive or negative?

1. Mechanics — machine process, use, development, design, or repair.
2. Scientific — process, analysis, scientific potentialities, development.
3. People — behavior, needs, causes, capacities, interests, activities, interrelationships.
4. Mathematics — compilation, computation, analysis, recording, projection, coordination of activities.
5. Records — historic, compilation, activities, background for action, sense of completion.
6. Art — creative, portraiture, record, expression, appreciation, symmetry, balance, discipline.
7. Literature — historic, review, support, reference, documentation, analysis, expression, communication, verbal artistry.
8. Sales — ideas, products, process, guidance, assistance, persuasion, communications, establishment of relationship.
9. Ecology — environmental, human interest, balance, recreation, relationship, abstract science, evolutionary influences, history.
10. Recreational — coordinated with other interests, abstract, relationship formula, indoor-outdoor environmental considerations, individual or coordinated effort, sociability or individuality, escape or involvement.

The Meaning and Impact of Interests

Used in early occupational guidance of young people, interest patterns have been found to remain fairly constant throughout the entire lives of men and women. Positive interests show areas and activities in which there will be positive support, and thus denote the particular spheres in which a worker's potentialities are greatest and are most assured. Insofar as possible, therefore, the occupation of the individual should be primarily composed of elements in which he has reflected positive interests. Actually, all of the positive interests of the individual should be encompassed in his occupation or in a combination of his occupation and what he does in his personal non-work activities.

Interest patterns reflect the specific nature of the worker's greatest potentiality. To some extent, the intensity of his interest reveals the degree to which he will actively devote his energies toward the development and fulfillment of the potential which is therein reflected. However, added influences — such as physical and emotional vitality, apathy or determination, general attitude (all factors which become evident through interview and observation) — also are essential considerations in estimating both the potentiality of the individual and the extent to which this potentiality may attain its maximum realization.

Assessing Your People Potential

The latent capacities and capabilities of people are enormous, beyond accurate estimate. And the experienced supervisory manager each day recognizes more and more of this potentiality — and of his own role in discovering it, defining it, energizing it, and applying it. Such exploration of the *direction* and *nature* of workers' potentialities is a first step: the next is to discover how these can be activated, developed, motivated, guided, and utilized.

By analyzing the specific nature of the interests and potentialities of the individual employee, the supervisory manager discovers what he can develop and attain with one worker. In the aggregate of his knowledge and understanding of *all* of the workers under his jurisdiction, and how he can inspire, motivate, and apply them, the supervisory manager can estimate and visualize his own "people potential."

You must know your people — understand their potentialities, as well as their present skills and talents. You must carefully assess how their potentialities match up to their current skills and their past experience. And you must understand the sensitivity, degree, and nature of the individual worker's differing responses and reactions to the physical and human-relations environment of work. Knowledge, understanding, and application of these factors are what help a supervisory manager to attain his people potential — and thus to achieve maximum value to his company, his employees, and himself.

2

HOW TO INCREASE YOUR UNDERSTANDING OF YOUR WORK GROUP

When I arrived one morning for a routine visit at Rogers Plastic Company, a New England manufacturing concern, the company vice-president, Henry Gangwisch, suggested, "Some sort of personal relations problem has come up between Gert Beaudry and Sandra Newton and it's lousing up our packing and shipping. You know them both; as an outsider, possibly you can help them to get it straightened out!"

I had known the ladies for 15 years or so and had a great deal of respect and fondness for them both. Sandra had served as an assistant to Gert for about 20 years, and had then been promoted to forelady of the warehousing department. Gert was forelady of the packing department. The two women necessarily worked and coordinated closely. So the fact that their personal and professional relationships had hit a snag had a serious impact on the subsequent operation of shipping, as well as on the proficiency of the departments they headed.

Talking with the two ladies individually, I discovered that a misunderstanding had arisen from a totally unintentional slight which Gert had infliced on Sandra. Sandra had approached Gert's desk at a time when Gert was deeply engrossed in discussion with a subordinate. Not noticing Sandra, Gert had walked away to another part of the packing room to take care of the problem she had been discussing.

Both women were too tense and too upset about it to deal with the problem calmly and unemotionally, and so, as time went on, the situation constantly worsened instead of getting better. Because they were personal friends as well as working colleagues, each woman desperately wanted the problem to be solved. Each woman was "completely willing to quit, if it would restore our friendship" or relationship.

A few hours later, the two ladies were working with their accustomed efficiency, effectiveness, and harmony. Yet my role was only that of an arbitrator, serving as a communications link between the two, reassuring each of the good will of the other. As any supervisor-manager would do in similar circumstances, I asked each lady what the problem was, why she was upset, indicated the good intentions of each, reflected to each how much her friendship meant to the other, and asked them both if, as a favor to me, they would have a cup of coffee together. I told each lady that the other was eagerly willing to apologize. Actually, my action in this case exemplified one of the most frequent "custodial" responsibilities of the supervisor-manager in developing the valuable relationship between the employees for whom he is responsible.

The Effects of Groups on Individuals

The most effective, dedicated, and personable training director I have ever known is a young man who, by himself, is meditative, shy, withdrawn, and possesses a great deal of private wisdom. This same man, in interaction with groups of people, becomes strong, dynamic, forceful, adroit, and inspiring. By contrast my father, a highly successful dentist and a man who inspired near-reverence in those who knew him personally and well, had an amazing capacity to project his gentleness, wisdom, strength, and sensitivity to people individually — and, somehow, to build the people's confidence in themselves. Yet with large groups of people, my father became shy, retiring, and virtually nonverbal.

The examples of this difference between people in individual and group situations are many and varied. Bernard Mack was an excellent machinist. In fulfilling his responsibilities as a machinist, he was cordial, friendly, thoughtful; he willingly and patiently undertook to train others in the occupation. Yet Bernard had been promoted and "set back" three times. It seemed that the moment he had supervisory responsibilities, he became overbearing, insensitive, irritable, and sarcastic.

In a different context, but an identical type of problem, the business agent of the union by which a client company was organized told me, "If you really want to do a service to this company and its people, you will make Fred Chatham (the president) recognize that the union members toward whom collectively he has such antipathy are the very same people toward whom individually he is so kind and thoughtful."

The union was well pleased with the contract which they had negotiated with the company, with the wage rates and provisions of fringe benefits and working conditions, and with the general atmosphere of the company and its overall attitude toward the union. However, the president, who was extremely well liked by individual employees, emphatically refused to sit in on any of the negotiations, responsibilities for which he delegated to other members of the management team. On the rare occasions when Mr. Chatham was forced to confer with groups of employees representing the union, he was "an entirely different kind of guy": he appeared belligerent, insensitive, demanding, and dogmatic.

Drawing an obvious but erroneous conclusion, the union business agent regarded this as an indication of Mr. Chatham's near-psychotic negativism toward the union and toward unionism. The truth was that Mr. Chatham's greatest self-confidence was in dealing with people individually; he had the feeling of being swamped when confronted with group debate. Mr. Chatham could handle speeches and monologues to groups of people with unusual expertise — but in the diversity and clamor of group debate, he became irritable and antagonistic.

Very often I have heard supervisors comment, "I don't understand this guy. In our individual relationship, he is friendly, responsive, and understanding, but put him together with other people and he becomes a belligerent rabble-rouser." Or: "By himself Joe seems lost and totally lacking in self-confidence. But he's a highly skilled worker: in his own job, and with groups of his peers, he's a real tiger." All of us have read enough about riots, revolution, and violent strikes to recognize that the chemistry of people in groups is very different from that of people individually.

What Makes Everyone Different

In other words, we often see people react in ways which we regard as out of character or actually contradictory to what we feel to be their basic natures. People are stimulated by other people — and the things which become most evident are their attitudes toward other people, and their images of themselves. Much of the stimulus which a worker exhibits in his relationship with others depends on the aptitude and efficiency with which a person feels that he performs in the activity which he undertakes with the group.

I remember watching a shy, withdrawn, double-amputee slowly and painfully move himself across a bathing beach and into the water. Once in the water, a remarkable transformation took place. Because of the compensated development of his arms, he was an unusually powerful swimmer; he suddenly became a dynamic, outgoing, and self-confident man, joining in all the games and recreations of the people around him.

From a very early age, we begin to formulate concepts of what work is like, and what it will mean for us and do for us — and how we will fit in and relate through our work. Later, when a choice has been made of occupation or profession, we develop an image of that profession and of ourselves within it.

One of the members of a Chicago workshop on engineering management reflected this when he said, "Sometimes you may think that a young engineer overestimates the importance of his field. But remember, engineering is a difficult qualification to obtain. There are long years of hard work, during which the only thing which keeps a man going is the fact that engineering and its profession are important to him. It's pretty rough to graduate, and then suddenly find that other people don't share the belief in its importance."

The supervisor-manager must always bear in mind that work must answer for an employee this question of his own self-worth, and that this will influence the worker's assignments and his attitudes toward people and jobs — how they are used, their skills are used, their efforts and skills are valued. In this case, engineering is what the young engineer has to contribute. And if he is made to feel that engineering is unimportant, he is made to feel that he, too, is unimportant. It's a terrific blow to his self-value and to his sense of security and future promise. Possibly it sounds a little rough to suggest that the supervisor must always reflect that he values the job, the employee, the skill, and the effort. But isn't it a respectable value? If it isn't, stop paying for it — and eliminate the job. If it *is* necessary, and it does contribute, respect the employee and appreciate his skill and effort.

Similarly, the papermaker learns his profession through apprenticeship and long years of sacrifice and effort. He has dedicated himself because he believes in the importance, prestige, and security of the occupation. His occupation is not only his source of income and interest — it establishes his way of life, and his sense of self-value. And he needs, in his occupational relationship, to have the importance he has ascribed to his occupation and his skill recognized; he must find it substantiated by the respect and appreciation reflected by his boss.

Employees' work-relationship needs, whether they pertain to the occupation itself, or, more generally, to the relationships which are coincidental to work assignments, must be studied individually.

Non-Occupational Work Considerations

It is often necessary for me to work directly along these lines with people, suggesting to them and to the companies that employ them the kinds of occupations, activities, and work environments which would be most favorable and suitable. For this purpose, certain well-known and simple psychological tests are used — partly to reassure the accuracy of what I am able to observe through discussion and interview, and partly to provide a degree of insight into people's interests and personality traits, which otherwise would take impracticably long periods of time to adequately study.

In one such review, I found apparently contradictory indications: a girl who had had very little basic interest in people, and was more inclined to withdraw than to be sociable, reflected a strong desire to work with groups of people rather than by herself. As it turned out, this was because she wished to "hide" in numbers of people — to be inconspicuous and undistinguishable within a group of people — and not for any tendency toward interrelationship or team effort. She was essentially shy and self-effacing. Her need was for impersonal relationships — and ones which were coincidental to work — rather than a status, product, or characteristic of an occupation.

Kevin Williams was a highly trained engineer. Despite the rapid promotional prospects which his unusual ability assured him, Kevin dedicated himself to outside studies in engineering to such an extent that it eliminated all time and energy for recreation and personal socializing. And to this he added such an intense "political campaign" that he made himself disliked and distrusted by both his co-workers and his superiors.

When Kevin ultimately hit the inevitable snag in his career project — was by-passed in a promotion which he felt he merited and for which he believed himself to be the most qualified and capable candidate — I had an opportunity to talk with him at length.

Kevin was one of the most hostile, egotistical, self-centered men I have ever known. He was striving for a corporate vice presidency. But this goal had nothing whatsoever to do with income potentialities and prestige, or the opportunities for him to develop people, or further his profession of engineering, or join in the growth of the company. Instead it was a personal vendetta. During Kevin's early high school years, his father had been fired "for just cause" by a manager at a subsidiary plant of the company. And Kevin was driven by a desire to attain a power position in the company, from which he could administer revenge.

What do people seek or need in occupational relationships? It is important to know, and to understand. And we can be seriously misled by generalities, superficial experiences, or our neglect of the needs and concepts of individual employees.

For instance, we might generalize that "membership" reflects a person's desire for interrelationship. This may be true of a social club, or of a religious organization, but is it true of membership in a union?

One person may need a group relationship in order to find his identity within the group. Another may need group relationship in which to hide or become unobtrusive. A third person may need group relationship in order to contribute his skills and efforts, and thereby to find a sense of purpose and self-worth. And a fourth person may need group relationship to cover up a sense of personal inadequacy, or to help him overcome a sense of weakness or inefficiency.

As these examples suggest, individual needs for relationship may vary so widely as to be opposite. Within the very same group, one man may feel that the relationship gives him purpose, meaning, and identity; while another feels, oppositely, that by membership in the same group he is surrendering purpose, meaning, and identity in exchange for the support he will obtain from the collective strength of the group.

The first of these two men would secure a sense of identity from precisely the same work situation which causes the second man to feel that he is losing his. In effect, the first man is selecting a group with which and within which he chooses to identify. His individual needs will dictate how he wishes to be identified within the group:

for example, as an inactive or inactive voice, a mere member, or its ultimate leader. And the second man reflects his feeling that to become a member of a group diminishes his individual identification and his prospects for it.

It is vitally important to understand the individual needs, concepts, and attitudes in work relationships. But when this is known, healthy relationships can be developed and can be made to fulfill an employee's needs — and group interaction can be understood and forecast.

Work as a Basis of Human Relationships

It is vital for us to know how an individual will react to the influences of working with others — and why. But beyond the effect of the group on the individual, we must next concern ourselves with teamwork, and the interaction of people working together. Many supervisory managers regard team-selection and team-building as the most complex and troublesome part of their assignments.

Every experienced supervisor-manager has, at some time, become discouraged at the difficulty of getting people to work together cooperatively, harmoniously, and productively. Sometimes supervisors are led to feel that work has the effect of eroding or complicating human relationships. Yet the truth is that mutual work effort and activity are not merely an aspect of human interrelationships, they are actually the basis both for forming human relationships, and for sustaining them. And the human needs of employees for work-based relationships make the supervisor's job one of the most challenging and potentially rewarding of all professions. Such mutual effort is the foundation not only for our working relationships, but for relationships in our private and personal lives, as well.

Let's take a hard, realistic look at what they variously call "human cohesiveness," collective effort, or teamwork. What brings people together? Very simply, it is mutual interest, common problems, or coordinated effort. A supervisor who makes a bad misstep in handling human relations problems in his department very soon learns teamwork and group effort in a negative way. People get together very quickly to work concertedly to his detriment.

But on the positive side, the constructive supervisor finds that he can effectively build work relationships and teamwork through identifying common needs and interests, and that once this is done, the process of working together continually strengthens the human bond. People actually relate and communicate by, as well as in, their process of working.

Work as a form of communication and a human bond of relationship was once illustrated for me by two children on the shore at Ocho Rios, Jamaica. As I watched, a little flaxen-haired girl and a strikingly dark-haired boy approached each other from opposite ends of the beach. They were about four years of age. It turned out later that the little girl spoke only in Swedish, the little boy spoke only in Spanish. They met, stopped about four feet from each other, and looked at each other intently for several moments, making no effort to communicate by words or gesture. Suddenly, as if by pre-arranged signal, the two children dropped to their knees in the sand.

For the next 30 minutes or so, the two children worked industriously together building a sand castle. Seeming to recognize the futility of words, neither child made any effort to speak. Even the communication of gestures was relatively infrequent. The sand castle completed, they arose, without gesture or attempt at words, and departed in the directions from which they had respectively come — without looking back, and without further effort to communicate. For these few moments, the two children from distinctly different parts of the world had met for the first time, had "related" for mutual interest, and had adequately communicated through the medium of occupation and shared effort.

Although I have read many fine books on this subject, I did not at the time fully recognize the significance of this experience in terms of supervision and supervisory management. As a matter of fact, it was not until a Pakistanian engineer expressed the same thing to me in terms of the complex world of politics and business that the fundamental meaning of this incident became fully clear to me. Just as is true in the world of adults, these children had been drawn together into teamwork and mutual understanding through work and effort. They understood each other in terms of a mutual interest and the occupations and skills which each had to contribute. The knowledge of what was to be done, and the interest in doing it, transcended their language barriers. These two children had demonstrated the soundest, securest, and most reliable basis for human relationship and understanding. They had thus reflected the tremendous value and potential of the supervisor-manager who appreciates work and skills as a form of human communication and teamwork relationship, and who thus can understand, build, orient, and direct employee relationships on the basis of jobs and assignments.

Work: The Basis for Relationship and Understanding

The Pakistanian engineer, attending a seminar which I conducted, suggested, "I think we're taking an entirely wrong approach to developing personal and international human understanding and relationships. We assess each other on the basis of how we differ, instead of how we resemble each other. For instance, we look at each other's religion, skin color, politics, language, and traditions: because we consider these things in which we differ, our potentiality for productive and harmonious relationship depends on the extent to which we are individually or mutually willing to ignore, adjust, or compromise these differences."

He was right: all of these are matters about which the average man has more emotions than knowledge. Therefore, they are things about which he is individually and collectively less flexible, less willing to compromise or surrender. To see what I mean when I say it is an area of emotions rather than knowledge, compare for a moment a man's attitudes and knowledge of politics, on which he spends a few hours each year, with his relative knowledge of his job, on which he spends about eight hours a day.

And this approach on the basis of differences is unnecessary; there are many ways in which we are similar in our values, activities, roles, or motivations. The engineer's point was that these similarities can serve as a common denominator of understanding. When we build our relationships on the basis of our similarities and resemblances, we will understand each other more readily, freely, and fully; and thus, instead of trying to compromise our differences, perhaps we can then foster them, enjoy them, and mutually profit from them.

It's not an entirely new idea, nor is it as complicated as it sounds. People often speak of engineering as an international language. Among engineers, there is an international language of formulas, diagrams, technical terminology — but more important, there is a sense of knowing and understanding each other because they are engineers and thus share interests.

The thought of this engineer from Pakistan was that *all* occupations can serve in a similar fashion. Jobs and community effort (sometimes referred to as "community of effort and interest") were the original basis of all society, and man's skills, efforts, and contributions were the basis of man's identification. And today, whether his nation and its industry are sophisticated or primitive, every man has a job or an assignment of some sort. Jobs essentially are the ways in which a man fulfills his responsibilities and relates to other people — how he applies his efforts and skills in terms of the needs and requirements of his family, community, nation.

I have often wished that I knew the name of this engineer because his idea has had profound influence on all of my subsequent work and activities. Actually his idea was the underlying reason for my lectures, visits, and discussions throughout much of Asia and the South Pacific. It has been fascinating how much I have found others — very different people, of many religions, political beliefs, skin colors — wholeheartedly affirming and accepting this concept. During visits to comparable manufacturing organizations in the United States, New Zealand, Australia, Malaysia, Thailand, China, the Philippines, Japan, Canada, I frequently have been asked questions by bench-workers, "How do they do this in other places you've been? Do the men work the same?" In all of my discussions with workers, I find a developing realization of the similarity and comparability of occupations and of people — and thus of comprehension and understanding.

How Occupations Form Relationships

When we speak of jobs, we refer to human efforts applied with purpose and direction. When we speak of teamwork, we think of the collaboration of people in joint effort; in so doing, we recognize that the team relationship is founded on mutual effort, direction, and purpose.

History reminds us that cultural units such as tribes and nations were initially formed to meet requirements for collective and coordinated effort, which men and women fulfilled through the jobs and assignments to which they applied their specific skills. People were brought together through the need for collective effort, and were bound together by the practice and relationship of that mutual effort. Occupations both formed and sustained human relationships.

In our present day, association and institutional leaders especially recognize and utilize this bonding effect of shared effort and occupations. Projects are often specifically designed to attract, build, and sustain the interest, involvement, teamwork, and support which are vital to the survival of such groups.

To most supervisor-managers, occupations and teamwork represent a major problem in human relationships. But this whole area of supervisory responsibility becomes a lot easier and a lot more interesting when a supervisor-manager recognizes that occupations by their nature are a form of human relationship, and in every sense are instruments for achieving human relationship and identification.

A detailed discussion on how jobs and work fulfill people's need for individual identity, self-purpose, and values belongs in our later section, dealing with employee motivation. But it is appropriate here to recognize the essentialness of work and effort as fundamentals of the bond of human relationship, affinity, and understanding. Work and assignments in themselves form the relationship of people. Responsibility of the supervisor-manager is therefore not to formulate relationships, but to assure that these occupationally formed human relationships are productive, meaningful, and harmonious, and are freely communicative between work people themselves and between work people and those to whom they are responsible in the performance of their assigned activities.

Because occupations do serve as the basis of people relating one to another, occupations serve as our identification to other people to a degree which we are more and more beginning to recognize. Identity needs of an individual, for example, can and should be fulfilled within the person's occupation. Supervisors often learn belatedly that they, too, are identified by others in relation to their occupation. And it is a serious error to ignore that identification in forming and developing relationships with subordinates. In effect, the supervisor who is overtly personal with his workers finds that he is out of character with the way in which he is identified by subordinates — and, thus, what they expect of him.

Sometimes the extent to which the role of jobs serves as a basis for human relationships, identity, and identification can be amusing. For instance, in seeking to clarify my occupational identity, a San Francisco audience member asked me at lunch break if I were employed full-time for the firm which was sponsoring the seminar. When I indicated that I was not, he asked me, "Then who do you work for?" I answered, briefly, that I worked for several seminar sponsors, was engaged by a number of companies as a management counselor, served as a speaker for a number of institutions and associations, and did a little writing in my free time. He looked at me silently; then, in apparent shock and disbelief, he muttered, "You don't have a job — you don't have a job!" And I could see from his facial expression, as well as his tone, that he had just concluded that I was unrelated to the human race because I did not have a recognizable full-time job.

Interpersonal Relations Between Your People

The fact that human relationships are established by jobs and work assignments suggests to us some of the motivational values with which people potentially may approach their work. When we also recognize the human requirement for relationship, we begin to realize the vital role which occupations can and must play in the personal and social, as well as the economic, lives of people.

Perhaps more importantly, so far as the supervisor-manager is concerned, we realize that the supervisor's responsibilities are largely for the development and custodianship of relationships with and between subordinates, rather than for initiating and formulating such relationships. Since occupations in themselves initiate and formulate employee relationships, the supervisor-manager's time and energies can be channeled into development and custodianship, where they are most appropriate and where they will do the most good.

"Don't think for a moment that this makes our relationship problems either easy or simple," a factory superintendent commented. "It's not easy — because you've got to learn what your people individually think is important, what their capacities are, and to govern your actions by this, rather than by your own ideas of values."

It's true. If we understand the potentialities which occupations have for formulating and sustaining relationships between workers, we can readily utilize and develop them in these terms among our employees. However, to do this effectivly, we must also be aware of the specific needs, capacities, or problems of our individual workers in relating to other people. Potentialities of relationship or problems of individuals can be highlighted by considering:

1. What are the worker's apparent attitudes and reactions to the prospect of working with others?
2. Does the worker have a capacity for relaxed conversation and communication with co-workers?
3. What is the general pattern of the worker's personal and social relationships?
   a) Does he have few or many friends?
   b) Are his personal and social activities frequent or infrequent?
   c) Are the social activities which he most enjoys structured (meetings, dances, outings) or relaxed, personal, and casual?
   d) Is he usually an officer, committee man, casual member, by-

stander, or inactive member of the clubs and social organizations to which he may belong?

4. In his prior employment or education, did he either engage voluntarily in team activity or find areas or reasons for working and cooperating with others?

5. If he is already an employee of the company, what appears to be his relationship with other people? And their attitude and reaction toward him?

Having thus predetermined the individual's compulsions or problems in relating to others, the supervisor's principal activity is in providing necessary orientation and introduction of the worker to his job, assignment, and co-workers. By these acts, a supervisor has prepared the groundwork for the relationship-building characteristics of work and occupations to have their full, effective influence.

Thereafter, as we have suggested, the responsibility of the supervisor with regard to the interrelationship of his workers is largely custodial in nature. And in this he will find that his initial care and studies stand him in good stead, not only in having placed relationships on the soundest possible basis, but also in providing him with information and understanding of the capabilities and potential problems of workers in their day-to-day relationships with co-workers.

The supervisor is thus able to avert the personal problem which we often encounter when we try to understand our people's relationship problems on the basis of strict rationality or logic. He is additionally fortified by knowledge of each individual employee. Without such individual understanding, we tend, too, to regard breaches of relationship or reasons which have caused them on the basis of our own ideas of importance or triviality. The fact is, however, the importance of problems of interrelationship must be assessed in terms of the values which people themselves place on them. And this is important to operations, because even a minor breach between two people — and one which has an apparently *trivial* underlying reason — can destroy the productive harmony and accomplishment of an entire plant.

Deliberate early effort in understanding workers' capacities and problems in getting along with others therefore pays off in two vital activities — the building of productive teamwork, and the sustaining of harmonious operations.

Occupations in Building Self-Expression and Work Relationships

Often we say that an artist — a painter, singer, poet, writer — is "expressive." This means that we recognize the capacity of such occupations to communicate, and that the practice of the occupation becomes a form of communication for the man or woman who performs the occupation. What we sometimes fail to recognize is that to some degree, at least, this applies to all occupations.

A young parking attendant with a serious and progressively crippling disability had admired a carved wooden dog that I carry in my car as a mascot. So I bought one and presented it to the attendant, incidentally mentioning that it was the last one that the carver had completed before going blind. His reaction was totally unexpected: "But what a memorial he has left for himself and his craftsmanship," he said. "To lose one's eyesight is bad — but not nearly so bad when talent and craftsmanship have made life so worthwhile. Think of the expression, the friendliness, the pleasure, and the beauty he has been able to give to so many people." And it made me feel how many of these same things the attendant had, without craftsmanship or skills, contributed to so many people in the course of performing his occupation.

Worker Communication Through Work

Recently, when I made a visit to a mid-west manufacturing firm, the plant superintendent stopped at a workbench and said, "Here — come here a minute: I want you to watch this guy. He's by far the best assembler we've got."

After watching the man's swift, adept fingers for several moments, I made a congratulatory remark to him. The man momentarily looked at me with a blank stare, then smiled, nodded, and resumed his work.

Manny, it turned out, could not understand a word of English; he was a Portugese national and the only Portugese-speaking person employed at the plant. He and his wife were also one of the very few Portugese families in the community. Because of his language limitation, Manny had initially been hired for a simple janitorial job, emptying waste baskets and discarding refuse.

Noting that whenever he had a few minutes to spare Manny would stand and watch the assemblers at work, the plant superintendent one day took him by the arm, led him to an assembly bench, and motioned for him to watch. When Manny began to relax, the superintendent gestured for him to take a place at the bench. Within the first 30 minutes he had gotten over his initial clumsiness; he made few mistakes, and by day's end he was keeping pace with all the others on the bench. He soon became the fastest and most accurate worker in the group.

When I spoke of the plant superintendent's thoughtfulness and understanding, he remarked, "Make no mistake: I've learned more from Manny than he has from me. For instance, he has taught me how much the relationship with and between employees is the responsibility of the supervisor or manager. Also he taught me how important both of these relationships are — how much both people and jobs depend on them and how much they, in turn, provide a fundamental form of communication."

Key Supervisory Responsibilities

Did you ever stop and enumerate our purpose in communicating? In the simplest terms, it is to make ourselves understood so that we can effectively motivate people, favorably inspire and coordinate their responses and skills. Actually, what a man says is unimportant — it is what is understood that's vital. And three of the most fundamental factors in effective supervision are:

1. Understand people in their own terms.
2. Let people know that they are understood in their own terms.
3. Communicate in terms that are fully understandable to the employee.

To be effective as a supervisory manager, it is thus essential to understand communication. It is vital to realize what it basically consists of, and to recognize why it is so infinitely important. Effective communication is fun, productive, and rewarding. The supervisor who understands communication — and who develops and applies it — gains for himself a vastly improved sense of well-being, and adds tremendously to his self-worth in his relationships and contributions to others.

To visualize, let's look for a moment at the effects of communication — and the needs. Although it varies in extent, as well as in nature and form, the most fundamental compulsion of healthy human beings is sociability: this is why we have been classified as "social animals." Thus, one of the most extreme of human needs is to relate to others. For some people, relationship needs are very restricted and easily satisfied. They may actually be limited to the immediate family, or to a few acquaintances, plus those purely routine relationships necessitated by community working and living. For others, obviously, extensive relationships are essential.

What Communicating Does for Relationships

What does this mean in terms of communication? Whether it is verbal or nonverbal, all relationships are necessarily and entirely founded on communication. In reaction to our initial need or desire to form a human relationship, we communicate in one way or another. And once the beginnings of relationship have been established, that relationship either improves or falls apart in direct relation to our effectiveness in communicating.

When we recognize these simple facts, it becomes obvious to us that what gives importance and purpose to communication is our compelling human need for relationship. In these terms, we can begin to understand the extreme personal problems of people who have difficulty in communicating. For instance, they feel very inadequate in their capacity to build and to sustain close and understanding relationships. Possibly the man who has difficulty in verbally communicating overemphasizes the importance of verbal ability, because he thereby feels inadequate. Such a person develops feelings of inferiority, and becomes hypersensitive about verbal insufficiency. And this, in turn, becomes magnified by the intense need for relationship and the feeling of being unable to achieve it. Then each human problem in the life of a verbally inadequate person reminds him of this communications deficiency, constantly intensifying it all the more.

The sense of well-being depends upon the capacity to communicate and relate, and inadequacy in this dangerously impairs a person's sense of self-worth and well-being. Nonetheless, some of the finest and most effective supervisors that I have ever known are men and women who initially had difficulty in verbalizing or communicating and thus had severe problems in establishing productive relationships. Because these folks themselves had had these difficulties, they could understand them in others, and could appreciate the uneasiness, despair, and self-worth questions with which verbally inadequate people are confronted.

Communications — Not Verbal Finesse

Effectiveness in communicating does not mean the glibness or expertise with which something is verbally expressed. The true test of communication is in the degree to which it is clearly understood by the employee and the extent to which the communication furthers relationship and understanding. Effectiveness in communicating thus depends on the supervisor's understanding of the individual employee even more than it does on his competence in verbally expressing himself and his ideas. Particularly those men and women who have had verbal problems themselves also recognize that the supervisor's understanding of the individual employee does much to make up for, offset, or diminish a worker's verbal deficiencies. Thus that individual's responsiveness and sense of self-worth, both personally and occupationally, are greatly improved.

A supervisor-manager's responsibilities are primarily the development and custodianship of relationships:

a) his relationship with his subordinates,
b) relationship of subordinates to work and assignments, and
c) relationship between subordinates.

And all of these are fundamentally and indisputably based on understanding and utilization of effective communications.

Understanding Employees' Reactions

The thing we must bear in mind is that the basis for people's understanding — and, thus, the way in which they will receive and interpret what we "communicate" with our words or actions — depends entirely on their prior experience, or what they have learned or been taught that something should mean to them.

To illustrate this, let's visualize two three-year old boys who are exactly the same in all respects except one. Imagine that these boys are exactly the same height and weight, have the same ethnic and nationality backgrounds — but that one was born in northern Alaska and the other in south Texas. Imagine that we rattle a couple of sticks: the boy from south Texas dives for cover, but the child from Alaska approaches with an expectant smile. Why? Because in the "language" of the child from south Texas, that sound means "Danger — rattlesnake!" To the boy from northern Alaska, it means a successful hunt, and a big meal forthcoming.

The identical communication can have opposite meanings. And so to do an effective job of communicating, a supervisor must recognize the different meaning which employees derive from his words and actions. Thus he must assure that both his verbal and non-verbal communications reflect to his employees what he wants his people to understand.

Sometimes I use a word interpretation to suggest this difference: for instance, the word "gopher" to the Minnesotan means a prairie dog, and to the Floridian means a land turtle. In all things, we interpret in terms of the meaning which we have individually learned. And whether it is in words or actions, the supervisor must understand the individual language of his employees and must communicate in these terms, in order to initiate and attain desired results.

Perils and Promises in Communications

As an elective project, a freshman at an eastern women's college chose a 30-day experiment in muteness. During this period, this ordinarily verbal girl was to use signs and gestures exclusively, and to completely avoid all oral expression. The result was a traumatic shock which required two years of recuperation to restore her mental and emotional equilibrium. As intense as the physical effect was on her unused vocal cords, this was by no means as severe as the impact on her mental and emotional health. She had put herself through the dual strain of reducing both her communications and her human relationships below their accustomed and required levels.

Humans require relationship and communication. Those who have impaired senses which make normal verbalizing and other communication impossible obviously adjust to other forms of communication and thus satisfy their basic needs. And use of alternative communications intensifies the senses which are thereby used, until, progressively, relationships can be amply formed and sustained.

But what of humans whose problems are insufficiencies rather than impairments? And how important is this on the basis of the volume and intensity of the average work group?

Generally speaking, in the average manufacturing concern approximately four out of ten non-supervisory workers verbalize adequately, and the remaining six have varying degrees of hesitancy or difficulty. Of course, among the four "most-outgoing" employees some will be found who are quite vocal and extroverted, and some who express themselves only when they feel a compelling reason to do so. Among the six "more withdrawn" people, some are merely hesitant to talk and some may have extreme difficulty.

Special efforts spent by a supervisor in formulating communications with those who have verbal difficulties are challenging — but it is also one of the most potentially satisfying aspects of supervision.

Foundry superintendent Carl Johnson utilized these principles wisely and well, applying the idea that occupation and performance are important aspects of communication, in developing communications rapport with an employee who had verbal difficulties. Carl set up a series of pre-planned private interviews with the employee. The first sessions were quite brief; later interviews became longer.

Carl carefully selected interview questions. The earliest were quite simple and direct; most of them could be answered by a nod or a shake of the head. Most of the subjects dealt with work history, preferences for certain kinds and aspects of work, whether the man preferred to work alone or with groups. Questions in later interviews were somewhat longer and more complex. For instance, Carl slowly and distinctly asked a number of questions about previous work, work and social preferences, reasons for initial selection of occupation, the occupations of other members of his family, the school status of his children — each phrased so that a few simple words would be adequate answer, or so that Carl could take over the verbalizing, in the event that the words were not forthcoming.

With the worker's original job application in front of him, Carl said: "I see that you worked in a production and repair department before you entered the machine shop. Do you like your present work? . . . Had you worked on the same kinds of machines we have here before you came here? . . . Of the four styles of drill presses we have, which one do you like best? . . . Is it because of its speed? . . . Does it bother you to have other people working as close to you as we do in our shop here? . . . Here are a couple of things I'd like to talk over with you when we get together again next Tuesday: is there any work you'd like to do in the shop that we can help you learn — and, if there is, how can we help?"

Noticeably, most of these questions still were of a nature that could be answered by "yes" or "no." Or they were control questions for which Carl already had a fair idea of the answers and which he could thereby verbalize, if the employee showed difficulty or hesitancy in answering. Carl was careful to avoid areas in which the employee might have an emotional response. He also avoided questions on which the employee might feel that he was being judged, trapped, or committed.

Carl was building verbal bridges in his relationship with the worker. What he did, in effect, was to substitute his own words for the ones which he felt the employee might himself use. Gradually, this seemed to give the employee confidence in himself and in Carl's sensitivity and understanding. Progress was slow, to be sure, and it started off with one hesitating word at a time. But the effort was extremely rewarding. The man became one of the most skilled and dedicated workers in the shop, and a strong bond of mutual understanding and loyalty was formed. Outside sources reflected there was a great deal of help to the worker personally as well. Word came back to Carl that there was a much better feeling of understanding in his home, and that he had become a much happier and more relaxed person.

Carl commented summarily, "He's given me a different idea of what it takes to be a supervisor. Years ago I would have said that one of the first requisites was verbal ability. But he now has developed enough — he makes himself completely and readily understood — and he is so sensitive that he understands others very readily. Frankly, he's the one I would now recommend as our top candidate for the next supervisory position that becomes vacant."

3

HOW TO UNDERSTAND THE INDIVIDUAL EMPLOYEE

A popular news weekly, in an article published several years ago, suggested that "psychological testing is like wire-tapping — it's an invasion of personal privacy." In a similar tone, government regulations decree that inquiries about gender and age, and other personal and ethnic distinctions, are illegal questions for pre-employment records. And a number of union officials have sought to bar annual performance reviews, which they regard as dossiers of incriminating evidence in employees' work-histories. Thus a supervisor-manager is apt to become confused as to the limit of the legality and tact of the questions he may ask *of* a worker, or *about* a worker.

The Issue of Personal Questions

So much is said about what should *not* be asked. Yet at the same time, virtually every article or book about supervisory responsibility insistently emphasizes that a supervisor-manager must *know* his workers, and must understand them sensitively and individually. Elsewhere in this volume I have suggested that one of the prime current needs of both companies and work people is the leadership which only supervisor-managers can provide and that this leadership must be based on sensitive understanding of each individual worker.

A supervisor inevitably reaches the point of questioning "How much can I legally and appropriately ask and learn about my workers? And by what means can I find out what I need to know?"

To confront the matter squarely, unless or until he learns all he needs to know about his workers, a supervisory manager cannot do his job, cannot meet his obligations to his company, and cannot fulfill his responsibilities to his workers themselves. Twelve fundamental responsibilities of the supervisor-manager's job depend on extensive knowledge and understanding of the following factors as they relate to individual workers:

1. selection
2. assignment
3. placement
4. orientation
5. reassignment
6. employee motivation
7. employee training and development
8. employee progress
9. employee relationships
10. performance improvement
11. setting and fulfilling of worker's occupational goals
12. employee counseling.

— From the Workers' Standpoint

Increasingly, certain occupational needs of workers are becoming intensified as, simultaneously, more and more of their personal and social needs are turning to work and occupational relationships for fulfillment. For example, worker needs for individual identity, values, sense of self-worth, sense of fulfillment, all are becoming increasingly job-related. Like the need for individual identity, fulfillment of virtually all of these worker-needs depends heavily on the specific, sensitive, and individual understanding of the worker by his immediate supervisory manager.

It all seems to add up to confusion and dilemma. And this confusion is still more heightened by two apparently contradictory reactions of the workers themselves. On the one hand, they are concerned about the current cataloging of people and the uncontrolled accessibility of personal information in both government and commercial data banks and computer centers. On the other hand, there is the worker's need for individualization and identity, which can be provided only by a sensitive and well-informed supervisor-manager.

Examine all of these protests closely and critically. As you do, you will find that each is based on fear. The concern is not for the information itself, or the privacy it suggests, but fear of how the information will be used or released. There is concern for the fact that the information may be misused, may become detrimental to the worker and to his best interests.

This implies suspicion. It reflects that those who fear the misuse of information about themselves or others, feel that they cannot safely entrust this information to those by whom it is sought. People feel that their greatest vulnerability lies in this private — and usually confidential — information; and they therefore feel that their well-being and defenses are at stake when they reveal it.

Mistrust Is Sometimes Justified

As I have suggested elsewhere, historic hiring practices were based on risk prevention rather than on current philosophy of human development. Information about workers and prospective employees in prior years was sought for the purpose of trying to pre-estimate the weaknesses and limitations of people and thereby to eliminate from further consideration any job candidates who were regarded as potential risks. Because supervisors of that period managed negatively, they sought this information for negative purposes — actually to be used *against* people, instead of *for* them.

In the most significant change which is taking place in management and managerial philosophy, we now manage *positively* instead of *negatively.* To phrase it in another way, we seek virtually the same information — but we obtain it to determine the *potential* of workers, rather than the *risk* they may represent. We try now to ascertain what they have which we can *build on* and *build with.* We need people, and we need to determine and develop their potentialities fully. In reality, this makes both employment and the availability of all personal facts and related data a matter of *mutual* interest between the supervisor and the supervised.

I have personally conducted thousands of psychological tests, and I have asked a great many deeply searching personal questions of many workers in various industries and businesses. Only once or twice, to this date, has any worker refused to undertake psychological tests or to answer any personal questions which have been asked. However, in recognizing the hesitancies and self-consciousness which may be involved, and the historically justified fears, I always make sure in advance that people know:

1. What the tests or questions involve.
2. For what reason the tests or questions are suggested.

3. What use will be made of the information which is thereby secured.
4. Who will have access to the information.
5. What effect the information will have on the person answering the questions or doing the tests.
6. What specific value the information may have for those who co-operate and participate.
7. When and how they will receive report of any results or compilations of information.
8. What control cooperating workers may have over scores and information, should they wish to exercise it.
9. What reciprocal cooperation they may receive in return for their participation.

Workers Respond to Constructive Attitudes

Although this is merely a personal experience, I feel that it is revealing of human nature and response that in recent years probably 25 percent of the workers who have cooperated with me in testing have subsequently requested that I conduct tests for all of their families. Sometimes this has included all adult members of large families.

I firmly believe that the primary value of psychological testing is to help people understand *themselves* objectively and in perspective. Most people who have cooperated in testing have voluntarily passed along copies of their test reports to their supervisors. However, whether or not they are informed of individual results, supervisors find the tests helpful: it has been well enough demonstrated that when people attain perspective on themselves they progress in recognizing their actual potentialities, and that they improve in their work attitudes and results. So the mutual best interests of company and employee are assisted by the test, whether the company thereafter receives reports of the results, or they are kept confidential by the participant.

This may raise some question as to how a psychological test can help a supervisor-manager when he receives no specific information in regard to a worker's test scores and the interpretations of meaning. "Having the test scores and data not only help me to understand the worker, but additionally create a sense of mutual understanding between us, when we are both familiar with what they reflect," supervisor-manager John O'Connell suggested. "However, part of a supervisor's function is to help a worker know himself and his potential. The worker's participation in psychological testing performs this function for us. Of course I feel that it would be best if we could know the results, and could participate in all phases of our workers' personal development. However, even when we don't actually know the test results and what they specifically reflect, I find that a worker is thereafter better able to discuss his interests and potentialities, and to participate constructively as we set up appropriate individual training and development plans and programs for him."

The Supervisor's Approach to Personal Information

When the supervisor-manager recognizes the reason for workers' hesitancy or hostility toward personal questions, he approaches his personal research quite differently. The supervisor's job is one of trust, and the experienced supervisor-manager recognizes that workers' trust is not something which can be demanded or expected, that it will not be given spontaneously, that it must be earned. The supervisor recognizes the intensive information and understanding he must develop in order to fulfill his managerial function and simultaneously provide the worker the identity, recognition, understanding, motivation, and development he needs *for* and *in* his job. But he also realizes that this data sometimes must be acquired gradually, sensitively, painstakingly.

Sometimes you get virtually all the data, feeling, and understanding you need in the first interview. Or sometimes you may find it necessary to parcel out parts of the interview. For instance, it may be necessary to have a job candidate talk to some of the other workers in the department, with whom he may feel more relaxed.

John Gansevoort, a rubber company production supervisor, reported, "With a real shy guy, it may take six months or more. At the time of hiring, you just get a few basics — and enough data to be able to place him on an appropriate job and with the kind of people with whom he will work best and easiest. Usually I then do the rest of my interviewing on the installment plan: I get him into the office maybe five or six times to chat, and I make a point of chatting with him periodically at his work place. I conduct performance reviews with all new people at the end of the first six months. I try to complete getting all of the basic data then; usually it works, sometimes I have to take longer."

What a supervisor-manager needs to know about each individual worker is basically the same as the information that has been sought by supervisors for many years. How this information is understood, how it is utilized, differs radically from past practice. But the outline is almost identical:

— background
— primary interest
— personal aspirations
— professional objectives
— self image
— personal circumstances
— capacities and work problems
— personality traits
— capacity to interrelate with others
— ability to communicate

All these same factors might be more illustratively listed:

1. Qualifications —
    education
    training
    prior work
    work experience
    work capabilities
    work problems
    ability to communicate
2. Human relations —
    personality traits
    ability to inspire favorable response
    attitude toward others
    capacity to interrelate with others
    attitude toward learning
3. Special "motivators" —
    primary interests
    personal aspirations
    professional objectives
    concepts of "how does it pertain to me?"
    self-image

Historic Questions — and Current Uses

With the exception of the self-image item — the importance of which we will explore later in the volume — the questions now are about the same as they have been for the last 30 years or more. The significance is in the way in which the information is understood and used. Typical of these is the difference between the prior and the current use of the identical item "background." Historically, information pertaining to a worker's background was used primarily to ascertain his qualifications or disqualifications: in other words, background was explored to assess the degree to which the employee had a type and degree of training and experience which a job required; it was secondarily utilized to examine factors which might have negative or disqualifying influences. Still used, of course, to examine an employee's qualifications for an occupation and work environment, background now is utilized as the beginning resource for reviewing and assessing the worker's potentialities, motivation, projected development possibilities, interests, and long-range occupational needs.

At the time of hiring and in the subsequent period of employment, a supervisor-manager studies the background of a worker in order to determine not only the immediate suitability of the individual for the work which is to be assigned and the environment of the department but also how the worker can be expected to react within the environment of work, and how his potential can be developed and realized by the work circumstances, activities, and conditions. In this, in a very practical sense, the supervisor-manager is utilizing the identical factors in the conduct of work and development of people that the behavioral scientist relies on for his theoretical analyses and conclusions.

Although the theories and conclusions of behavioral scientists vary somewhat — and also are changing, as new studies are conducted — there are a few general conclusions which bear dependably and importantly on achieving effective results in supervision. In a general way, for example, we know that employees' response and behavioral patterns are the net effect of their underlying personalities, together with their understanding of situations and circumstances, when stimulated by the situations and circumstances in which they find themselves. In other words, a supervisor's beginning study and understanding of a worker is based pretty much on a formula: A (basic personality pattern) plus B (conditioning and learning) plus C (environmental influences) equal D (worker response and behavior). When first faced with a formula of this nature, a supervisor-manager often feels that his technical and operating responsibilities and his human relations responsibilities are separate, distinct, and often imcompatible. But actually this formula brings the two together into focus and consistency: production and output, which are the specific objectives of the technical and operational aspects of his job, are the direct result of human behavior and response, which are the supervisor-manager's objectives in human relations. In effect, a company's product is a tangible form, as well as a result, of human behavior and response.

Theories differ as to the extent to which basic personality pattern is inherited or is learned in early life. Some believe, for instance, it is controlled by human genetics or other prenatal considerations, where others believe that it is the result of early conditioning in the life of a very young human being. And opinions also vary somewhat as to which personality traits are basic and which are learned manifestations of an individual's values and feelings. However, these scientific uncertainties are, relatively speaking, details, and do not affect or diminish the usefulness of the "A plus B plus C equal D" formula in assisting supervisor-managers' study, observation, and understanding of people.

All of us know, for example, that the basic personality of an individual has a tremendous effect upon the degree to which he will happily and comfortably fit into the environment of work, its conditions and its requirements. An extreme introvert — a shy, withdrawn, unsociable individual — will obviously have greater difficulty and discomfiture in adjusting to a public-oriented occupation in sales. He can adjust to it, if he wishes, but in effect he will be running contrary to his basic nature. Similarly, a gregarious, extroverted, outgoing type of person would have considerable difficulty adjusting to a one-man research project on an isolated island. The supervisor-manager examines the basic personality pattern of a worker to determine how comfortably, happily, and relaxedly he will fit the conditions of an occupation and its requirements. Knowing that the personality characteristics of an individual worker will be accentuated or modulated by the suitability of a work environment, the supervisor-manager studies the personality characteristics of the individual to determine what will "bring out the best," what will "bring out the worst," and what conditions, circumstances, and relationships will do most to stimulate, motivate, and assure the happiness and comfort of the worker.

The Meaning of "Conditioning"

We additionally know that whatever the basic personality pattern consists of, it is accentuated, clarified, and directed in the subsequent step of human development, "conditioning."

We also know that in the conditioning process, which starts immediately at the time of birth of the individual, values, concepts, interest, pace, and language begin to become implanted and developed. Work motivations are not themselves developed in this youthful period, but the patterns of taste, needs, and values upon which motivations and interests are ultimately based commence then to take shape. And so to know a little bit about the home, school, community, and parental factors which condition people in their early youth, helps a supervisor to understand a little of their interests, motivations, needs, and conflicts.

It is necessary to know about people's values and interests in order to properly place and assign them. And this is even more essential to the worker's best interests in providing for his motivations, development, progress, and achievement, than it is to the company. For the employee this is the whole foundation of his sense of self-worth, value, and fulfillment. So far as the company is concerned, it is important, but primarily a question of degree in quality and productivity, effort, and accomplishment.

In his excellent book, *Developing Woman's Potential,* Edwin Lewis provides several illustrations of the importance of understanding this early conditioning in order to understand people themselves. For instance, most of us see traces of it in the play into which little girls are guided, and the toys — the dolls — with which they are provided. This is an education and a conditioning toward child-bearing, child-raising, and the cultural roles of domesticity and motherhood, and this childhood guidance significantly influences the attitudes, roles, and values with which women mature. It suggests to women a primary value and preference for motherhood — which, in effect, places occupational activity second in their preferences, motivations and responses.

The Importance of Understanding

Much of the job of supervision consists of matching interests and motivations of workers — as well as their qualifications — to the present and future prospects of an occupation. Therefore, as a supervisor, you will find that your general knowledge of the background and values of the worker can play a very important part in helping you to achieve full effectiveness in understanding and attaining your maximum "people potential."

Both positive and negative information have a constructive part to play. A few writers recommend that a supervisor-manager should review and discuss only the facts about which a worker is readily willing to talk. The thing that is wrong about this idea is that knowledge of other "negative" facts can help a supervisor to guide a worker away from a repetition of experiences which caused him problems in the past. A supervisor-manager can try to avoid creating situations which bring out the worst in a worker when he more fully understands a worker's history and the things which had previously incurred trouble for him. Most often the very things about which a worker is hesitant to talk represent subjects and situations with which the sensitive supervisor-manager can be most helpful to the worker, in guiding him in his development and work activities. And often the "hidden" information about a worker is vastly less significant than the worker has believed it to be, or it has no bearing at all on the new work situation, a factor which is particularly helpful for the worker to realize.

As Alvin Howe, machine shop foreman in a Philadelphia company, rather forcefully expressed it, "Negative facts about a man show where he's had problems. My attitude is that if a guy's had a problem, he may need help — and I can't help him unless I know the problem. If the problem was something temporary, and the cause and reason have passed, we can forget it. Sometimes you find that the guy learns most where he's had a problem, weakness, or failure. Once he faces it, with help and guidance, this can become his greatest strength and capability."

It all boils down to a basic question as to whether or not you are constructive, understanding, and responsive as a supervisor-manager. Where workers learn that the boss is understanding and responsive they, in turn, respond. They not only unhesitatingly answer questions, provide all the information that the supervisor needs, but also become responsive to his understanding, guidance, and leadership.

The supervisory manager who will not use confidential data about his people constructively, understandingly, and with discretion has no right to this privileged information. But such a man has no right to the position or authority of supervisory management — and he will be ineffective in his assignment, because he will be unable to develop the worker-responsiveness, support, and understanding which are absolutely essential in the fulfillment of his responsibilities.

Whether or not a supervisor-manager should seek personal information from or about a worker is not the real question; instead it is:

1. To what extent has a supervisor developed rapport with the worker?
2. What useful purpose will the information serve?
3. Has the supervisor allowed time for the worker to develop understanding and trust in him?

4. Has the supervisor given the worker adequate examples of how constructively he uses and safeguards confidential information?
5. Is the supervisor-manager objective: is he sure that he will treat all data with understanding, and not be "judicial" or "shocked"?
6. How will the information be used — and when?
7. Will the supervisor exercise total discreetness and not divulge information?
8. Does the supervisor-manager restrict his questions to those which have direct or indirect bearing on the work, attitudes, interests, responses, and potentialities of the worker?
9. Does the supervisor also allow time and attention for non-work-related information which the worker feels he needs to communicate?

The Effect of "Knowing"

As a supervisory manager, you soon discover that a great deal of your confidence in your people depends on how well you know and understand them. And you find that without broad understanding of an individual employee, you have misgivings and reservations. In effect, the extent to which you are responsive and rely on a worker depends upon the extent to which you know and understand him. Or, stated in opposite terms, the degree of your reservations and hesitancies about a worker directly relates to your limitations in knowledge and understanding of him.

Your degree of understanding of the worker — and thus, obviously, the inclusiveness of your knowledge of him — are essential in your attainment of your people potential, and in your assistance to a worker in achieving his maximum potential.

Some people believe that supervisory managers' information about their workers should be restricted purely to work qualifications. Such people believe that supervisors' knowledge and understanding of a worker's background, experiences, and problems establish a rigid mold and seriously restrict a worker's assignments and career.

The truth is that an experienced supervisory manager does not use this information negatively, to set limits and restrictions, but positively, to see from a worker's prior experiences and problems what he has to build on — and to build with. He examines every aspect of a worker's background with the question "why?" He tries to understand the influences, circumstances, conditions, and problems surrounding a worker's prior record, and how these may have contributed to his favorable and unfavorable experiences. For instance, if he discovers previous conditions which interest and stimulate a worker, he looks for these or tries to create them in the job or in the work environment. On the other hand, if he discovers circumstances which have adversely affected the worker, he tries to understand *why* they have had this effect. If the previous problem has been because of misunderstanding, the supervisory manager tries to achieve necessary understanding. But if it is something which just basically upsets the worker, the supervisory manager tries to avoid exposing the worker to its influences.

Knowledge Equals Something to Build With

You, as an experienced supervisor-manager, know that the conditions and circumstances of work — or of the working environment — stimulate people. This stimulation has the effect of bringing out the best or bringing out the worst in each of us. Because you are responsible both for output and for the harmonious relationship of people working under your jurisdiction, it is obvious that you will do a great deal of thinking about work environment, about conditions of work, and about how you can favorably influence your workers. And you must know your people to know what will influence them — and *how.* You also must know your people and understand how to build a productive climate of work in your department.

When you understand the underlying reasons for workers' behavior problems, you begin to see how often bad experiences reflect merely temporary influences in the personal lives of your workers. And you also see many times that negative work records have been caused by circumstances which do not exist within your company or department. In other words, your knowledge of privileged personal information provides you greater latitude and enables you to be more lenient than you would be if you were compelled to rely merely on "the record."

As an illustration, "the record" indicates merely that Frank Caswell was convicted and sentenced for larceny. But as office manager Ralph Payne interviewed him and delved into personal and privileged information, he discovered that Frank had stolen money while under desperate financial circumstances and the pressure of family illness. Ralph hired Frank and put him in a position of financial trust.

"If the guy had been convicted of embezzling company or bank funds, or if the reasons in back of the theft were such things as compulsive gambling, I might have taken a different tack," Ralph Payne explained. "But there was nothing in his case that really pertained to work here — and the outside factors that influenced him to steal no longer exist. He's a basically dependable guy; and, really, he's all the more dependable because he's trying to prove something to himself, as well as prove something to other people." At the time I knew about the case, Frank had done so well that he had been promoted several times, and was in an assignment in which there had been no problem securing the bonding coverage that was required because of his extensive responsibility for company funds.

The potentiality of people lies not in what they have done — or even, necessarily, in what they think they should do, or aspire to do. As is true of work record, aims and aspirations may be overly restricted because of the limitations in prospects and possibilities about which a worker has learned by his own experience.

— A Special Contribution

Your sensitive and comprehensive understanding of your employees gives dynamic possibilities to your use of your people potential. Additionally, the fact that this information has been mutually shared and known — and your understanding and responsive interest have been demonstrated — has a tremendously beneficial effect on the responsive human relationships between yourself and your worker.

Obviously, when you know your workers' potentialities and limitations, you more effectively attain your people potential. Also, you are more relaxed and sure of your operations and of your human relationships.

Consider, too, the strengthening effect your constructive attitude, knowledge, and understanding have on the worker and on his sense of well-being and self-assurance. When a worker withholds information, he does so primarily with the thought that its divulgence might be detrimental to him. Thus, he becomes furtive and guarded in order to assure that the information will not be revealed. He becomes tense and defensive, and inclined to increasingly exaggerate the potentially negative effect of the information, until his fear is beyond all reason and rationality.

Most often the things about which he is hyper-tense actually are rather trivial. So when these facts have been revealed with no harm-

ful effects, the worker becomes more realistic as to their significance, and more natural and relaxed in his work habits and work
relationships.

The fact that the information is known by his supervisor with no
disastrous effects is, to the worker, a reflection of the understanding and constructive attitude of his boss. And the fact that the information is not divulged or misused is an indication to the worker of
his supervisor's discretion and reliability. Information thus and then
becomes a common bond in the area of mutual understanding. It is
one of the strongest foundations for responsive and constructive
human relations.

A Summary of Thoughts and Considerations

Perhaps the most significant of all changes which have taken
place in management in the past 15 years is the alteration of the
responsibilities and stature of the job of supervising. This change
is and *reflects* all that is new in industrial objectives and viewpoints.
The job of supervising has changed from that of overseeing equipment and machine tenders to one which primarily deals with human
relations, human development, human reaction. Supervision is the
"human linkage" of the corporation.

Now and in the future, the success of corporations will depend
in enlarged degree on the human relations aptitudes and attitudes
of their supervisory people. And the success of supervisory people
themselves, in turn, will necessarily depend upon the sensitivity,
interest, positivism, and expertise which they develop in handling
people problems.

The success potential of a supervisor thus now is something infinite and incalculable. Back in the good old days of early American
industry — when a supervisor was hired to oversee the operation of
equipment — potential of a supervisor was very clear. Quite simply,
it was whatever percentage of machine capacity he could attain,
through avoiding breakdowns, down-time, and other equipment
problems and failures.

Always remember that now, as a supervisor, your potential is
not just your own skill and talent, or that of the machines you are
able to operate. Instead it is the aggregate or sum of the potential
of all your people. This is not just a simple formula of person plus
person plus person — but becomes multiplied, rather than added,
in the dynamic and amplifying effect which people have on each
other. And it is also magnified by the extent to which you can recog-

nize the talents of others — to develop them, motivate them, apply them, and guide them toward their own self-realization and fulfillment.

People potential is the most valuable asset and aspect of the job of the supervisory manager. People potential is something which we must recognize and measure by sensitive knowledge and understanding of people, of their backgrounds and experience, and of the reasons, rationale, and influences affecting them. People potential is something which demands that a supervisor have sensitivity, understanding, and vision — that for the mutual benefit of worker and company, he is able to identify the employee's potentiality, and visualize how it may best and most fully be utilized.

People potential is "turned on," activated, and motivated by positivism and leadership, by the understanding, sensitivity, and constructive attitude which a supervisor shows toward his people. A great deal of your attitude and sensitivity is revealed in your review of workers' backgrounds, capabilities, and potentialities. When they see in this and in you an attitude of positivism and understanding, they respond in these same terms. As a supervisor, you need to know your people — for your benefit and theirs. People are actuated by positivism; monotony and boredom are activated by negativism.

How to Make a Job Interesting —
and a Worker Responsive

You must know people sensitively and well, in order to learn what they value and need. And you must know these things before you can effectively "turn on" their efforts and interests; you cannot rely on your own concepts or "best guesses."

There's hint of a great truth in the humorous parable of the mid-eighteen-hundreds, which reads: "'There's no accounting for other people's tastes,' said the old lady, as she kissed the cow." The supervisory manager who tries to understand or pre-estimate people in terms of his own interests, tastes, or objectives soon finds himself up to his ears in a crucial problem of misunderstanding his people.

John Case, a master design-draftsman, learned this truth rather quickly when he took over as the new supervisor of a three-unit drafting department. One of the departmental units worked within the plant engineering area. A second unit, because of some outside contact, was located in the front office area. The third unit was used primarily on customer designs and problems, and thus centered most of its activities in customer plants and offices. John at first was terribly confused because he found that several worker-requests for transfers from one unit of the department into another were for reasons identical to the reasons stated by other draftsmen in explaining their desire to be transferred *out* of that particular unit.

John learned — as all experienced supervisors sooner or later recognize — that what people seek in a job and in a workplace is an individual and personal matter. It is precarious for you to try to "best guess" what an employee will most enjoy, or to judge from your own values what nature of occupational activity will best enable a worker to derive a sense of interest, satisfaction and fulfillment. And actually there is no need for "best guessing"; it is more reliable and far easier to observe and to ask questions. Such questions, as reflections of honest effort on your part to understand your people, do more than merely assist in securing information and understanding for you; they inspire favorable response on the part of your people, who actually are *seeking* to be understood. And the answers themselves are vital to you if you hope to be accurate and motivational in your understanding, assignment and management of people.

What people need to feel in a job is equally an individual matter. Helen Ames was a highly competent high-speed typist until an accident to her right hand mangled the bones beyond repair. This disabled her for all future typing — and this was an occupational capability on which Helen based a great deal of her self-image, identity and sense of self-worth.

Fortunately, after Helen had spent several dissatisfied years in filing and routine clerical work, a supervisor-manager recognized her need to work independently in a routine machine-assisted occupation, one in which she could progressively note tangible volume results from her efforts. Accordingly, he assigned Helen to a computer-function, in which she became intensely interested and highly successful. From the standpoint of his own tastes, interests and values, the supervisor-manager would have been bored with the routine, repetitive work. Because of this, he all the more appreciated and utilized Helen's avid interest in such an assignment, and demonstrated respect and esteem for the work she performed and the zeal with which she did it.

The self-values and self-expression which the individual employee finds in an occupation very often seems to lack logic; and superficial appearances, as well as your own ideas and preferences, can tend to mislead you. As a case in point, Mrs. Jane Woolner was a very personable, efficient, and successful waitress; her income was good, and she and her husband had been able to buy a house and quickly pay off their small initial mortgage.

But Jane was far from satisfied with her occupation; it did not give her what she needed to derive. Previously she had worked as a countergirl. Despite its lower rate of pay, Jane had immensely liked the job and had been satisfied in it: for some reason she had taken great occupational pride in having the wrist strength that enabled her to scoop hard ice cream with a cold scoop in a single arm movement. A fall and a badly broken wrist had made it necessary for her to change her occupation to one in which she did not find an equal sense of pride, and unique self-worth.

Very often some aspect of job pride and job interest relates itself to some characteristic of work in which a man or woman feels unusual proficiency. It is impossible to know what this is, *why* it is, or what it consists of without first knowing employees well, sensitively and individually. And when such facts, interests and worker directions are known and understood, it not only enables the development of the most mutually fruitful relationship between the worker and his job, but it also assists in averting negative circumstances, consequences and work assignments. In its positive sense we talk about motivation and productivity; in the negative sense we talk about fatigue, boredom, monotony, and our current efforts to correct these conditions through "job enrichment."

Treating Problems of Monotonous Work

As is true in the studies and efforts that are necessary to motivate people, to insure and highlight motivational aspects and ingredients in jobs and to develop effective leadership of people, you must carefully explore your workers' individual tastes and values before you take any action in assessing occupational monotony and workers' boredom. Work planning for motivation or to reduce monotony and boredom must be done on the basis of the specific evaluation and reaction of the individual employees who are affected.

One of the most effective means for attaining, assuring and maintaining this kind of sensitive understanding is through soundly conceived performance appraisal. In hiring a new employee, you go to extreme lengths to review and understand his abilities, experience and interests. When you are not satisfied that you have acquired all the necessary information at this time, you carefully continue your explorations until you believe that an adequate amount of data has been accumulated. But what of the subsequent period, after you have been initially satisfied in your understanding? Your observation and study of individual employees should continue — but do they? Most often you become diverted to other more pressing problems.

Well-conducted employee performance appraisal does many things: it places emphasis on the importance of doing the job; it clarifies and substantiates the value of doing the job well; it gives support to the value which the worker places on his occupation and his effort by reflecting that these things are valued by the boss, too. It highlights the greatest and least of the employee's talents and contribution — encouraging the perpetuation of his favorable performance, and guiding his improvement in the aspects of the job in which he has not done so well.

But most important of all, the annual appraisal interview is a time specifically set aside for the constructive discussion of job, job interests, needs, responses, aspirations, motivations and work values. It is a time when the supervisor and his subordinate spend time together mutually trying to improve the work relationship — mutually trying to make the work and its future fit the needs, interests and motivations of the worker, and the work and worker fit progressively and promotionally to the needs and interests of the company.

Thus, because they assist in developing updated understanding of your workers, annual job and performance appraisals with individual employees are one of the most effective means by which you can get to know your people well enough for you to analyze their needs in either motivation or the correction of boredom. However, problems arise at a rapid rate, and problems of such sensitive nature tend to become magnified when they coast along for periods of time without being resolved. Interim action is often essential. So, for this purpose, brief interviews and twelve simple questions, geared to understanding your people and their relationship to their assignments, can be extremely revealing and useful:

1. How do you like your present job?
2. How long have you worked at this particular job?
3. Before coming into this department, did you work at the same occupation in another part of this company, or in another company?
4. How did your assignment and job activities there compare with what you are doing here?
5. Are there aspects of your job here that you like better than your previous work? What are they? Why do you like them better?
6. Are there things which you liked better about your previous work? What are they? Why did you like them better?

7. What do you like best about your present job? Why is it that you like this?
8. What do you like least about your present job? What aspects of this particularly trouble you? Why?
9. If you had complete freedom to pick any occupation, what kind of a job would you select? Why? What particular thing would you seek in the job?
10. If you could pick any kind of work environment and any kind of work situation, what would you particularly look for?
11. Do you find other workers here friendly, helpful and responsive?
12. Do you have any suggestions which you might make as to how we might improve:
    — your job?
    — the department?
    — relationships within the department?
    — the pleasantness of work?

Distinguishing Boredom, Monotony and Fatigue

It is vital to bear in mind how markedly — contrastingly, perhaps — other peoples' values, interests and capabilities vary from your own. Because whether or not jobs and assignments will be boring or interesting, monotonous or suitable, depends on the interests and values of the people themselves — and *not* on your interests or assessments. Two things govern: the suitability of the assignment to the interests and capabilities of the worker; and the degree to which your attitude enables the worker to find and fulfill his self-value in the work. To put it bluntly, it depends primarily on your capability and wisdom in selecting and assigning people, and on your leadership and interest in people and work — how you continue to conduct yourself and your department.

If careful selection is undertaken and sensitive effort is devoted to assigning people as closely as possible to their interests, capabilities and potentialities, a great deal of the problem of monotony, boredom and fatigue is eliminated. And it is only after such careful consideration that clear and valid analysis of boredom and fatigue problems can be conducted; until that time, many of the problems which appear to reflect fatigue and boredom may actually be inadequate employee understanding, poor selection, or unwise assignment and administration.

For instance, such occupations as assembly and packing require a high degree of manipulative dexterity and coordination of eyes and fingers, but entail a very limited amount of judgment and discernment. In other words, such occupations do not heavily involve the mind. Among appropriately selected personnel, the lack of mental involvement reduces the likelihood of boredom. But among poorly selected people — and those who have a high requirement for coordinating thoughts with their physical activities in an occupation — boredom can become intense and serious.

On the one hand, cumulative fatigue rather than boredom is the occupation problem in such assignments as assembly, packing, typing, when personnel selections have been carefully made. Boredom is a problem on these occupations when worker assignments have been made unwisely, but the boredom is a selection problem, rather than an occupational problem. Occupational boredom is in the repetitiveness of what the job consists of. When personnel selection is handled poorly, boredom is incurred by what an occupation does *not* contain — by the failure of the occupation to provide for the specific needs of the worker.

Although this may seem like splitting hairs, it actually concerns one of the most fundamental considerations in discovering and treating monotony and boredom. Fatigue is combated one way, boredom another. Occupational fatigue is treated by rest periods, reduction in time-continuity of work, and sometimes by alternatives of physical position or finger-motion requirements. Boredom must be treated by creating diversity, adding different natures and levels of mental activity.

Sometimes We Learn from Necessity

An Ohio company negotiated a work contract in which one of the stipulations pertained to its policy on personnel selection. Under the contract, all hiring specifications and standards could be retained if their appropriateness and need could be substantiated and documented. The result was a significant moderation in the company's education requirements.

Discussing the experience, a supervisor-manager commented, "We had previously demanded high school graduation, or technical school certification, or college graduation for various assignments in the company. In many of our semi-skilled and unskilled occupations we are now staffed with people who have sixth, seventh, or eighth grade education. Our productivity is way up, our absenteeism and turnover are way down; I can only conclude that we previously invited boredom, disinterest, and poor morale by hiring over-qualified people, that people felt their jobs were pulling them backward. Now we have people who have to work up to their jobs — and in finding a sense of progress and development, they are challenged, interested, and motivated."

Useful Application of the "Think Tank" Concept

While many of the approaches to reducing monotony and boredom include some form of diversification of interest and activity, "involvement" ranks high among the most effective remedies. As we have discussed elsewhere in this volume, people are stimulated by people: relationship with others is an important primary motivation; an occupation can and should be a form of expression and identification for those who seek it in their work.

Boredom can result from a feeling of isolation — or a lack, in an occupation, of interrelationship with other people. Thus, for people who need relationship with others and fail to find it in their work, interaction with other people, regardless of how it is provided, assists immensely in alleviating problems of boredom.

The "think tank" approach can be extremely helpful in this "people interaction," as well as in other activities for which it is used. In participating in this activity, most people develop actively helpful ideas; and even in those whose role is more passive the participation is valuable, because it develops in them a keener awareness of the problem of their company, department, and occupation.

Realistically, company problems are by no means restricted to any one level of the company, but affect all levels. So the agenda of the "think tank" group discussions can be geared to the specific levels with which people have day-to-day working familiarity — and in the specific nature of related problems, can produce meaningful and useful thoughts, ideas, and suggestions.

Such interaction also helps to bring out and develop people, through the stimulation of working and relating with others. This provides an additional opportunity to observe the employee, and to demonstrate to the worker aspects of his potential about which he was not previously familiar.

The "think tank" activity, or some comparable form of interaction with other employees, thus is useful in enriching the employment and the work environment of workers whose occupations do not provide adequately for their needs in work relationships. At the same time they both bring out and develop the capacities and communications abilities of the worker. And they provide an excellent opportunity for the supervisor-manager to better understand the worker in terms of his relationship needs, communications problems and capabilities: in other words, to know the worker better and more sensitively in terms of these vital aspects of employee motivation.

Solution Is an Individual Matter

Each supervisor-manager should routinely conduct objective reviews of the qualifications of people and the appropriateness of their assignments to assure that both requirements and assignment are sound and accurate, and that prior specifications have not become obsolete. But beyond this, the questions of stimulation and boredom, like most supervisory considerations, depend on the supervisor's understanding of each individual worker. Apart from the very general factors of qualifications specifications, work assignments and distribution, and work environment, the factors of monotony, boredom, and disinterest must be separately considered in relation to each individual worker. In such a review a supervisor-manager first evaluates work, assignment, and the environment of work, to see what generally negative influences exist in the department, its work load, and its assignment — what features of work may detract from the effectiveness of his efforts to motivate his people. And finally he investigates how these things pertain to, affect and influence individual workers themselves. In this evaluation, you should:

1. Review and authenticate skill and qualification requirements of the department and its workers.
2. Establish occupations by grouping needs into comparable skills, degrees, and levels of skills.
3. Compute the number of workers needed at each skill-level by dividing the work load of that level by the expected daily accomplishment of each worker.
4. Select workers on the basis of qualifications to meet current operating requirements.
5. Plan and program for estimated future skills by developing and training, or by recruiting at the time of actual need.
6. Determine the skills, interests, potentialities, aims, aspirations, and work expectancies of each individual worker.
7. Assign and orient workers insofar as possible in terms of individual skill, interest, and motivation.
8. Identify the factors of work, work prospects, and work environment as they relate to the individual's needs, interests, motivations, and aspirations.

9. Maintain a continuing audit of the responses, interests, and accomplishments of each individual worker as they relate to his performance.
10. Conduct periodic personal reviews with each worker as to the progress in work, skills, performance, and toward the attainment of the worker's goals and fulfillment of his motivations and expectancies.
11. Appreciate your people and their efforts.

4

HOW TO BE UNDERSTOOD
BY YOUR PEOPLE

"Is there something about being a boss that makes a man automatically and inevitably disliked and resented?" asked a construction superintendent. To anyone who has ever been in a profession requiring self-discipline — or in which discipline is largely self-imposed — the answer is clearly "yes." Or, for that matter, to anyone who has ever had a fit of temper toward the morning alarm clock, the answer is clearly affirmative. After all, we set the clock — we have accepted the discipline of being awakened to do something which we believe is important or valuable to us. But we still resent the regimentation and discipline represented by the alarm clock.

Workers' Reaction Toward Supervision

As a supervisor you must accept this, and understand all that it implies. As mentioned earlier, a lot of supervisors get tripped up on this particular point. They feel too personally about it, and therefore take their jobs too personally, as well. Aware that their work force feels resentment toward discipline, less-experienced supervisors are apt erroneously to interpret this as meaning that they are committing some sin in the way they are conducting themselves. They therefore try to change either themselves or the rule, standard, or discipline.

There are two vital factors which you as a supervisory manager must always keep in mind. First is that your job of supervision reduces the personal aspect of your relationship with your subordinates. Necessarily you will be regarded primarily in the role of supervision, and all that this represents to your workers. Secondly, you must bear in mind that there are aspects to the role of supervision and leadership which subordinates will inherently resent. One of these is discipline.

This is inevitable. It is also impersonal. Very often it reflects inner conflict of the employee himself, as he struggles between natural inertia and the compulsion to act on something which he himself wants and has freely committed himself to do.

Here's a thought that may be useful for you to remember. All of nature is a balance between inertia and action; for every compulsion toward action or motion, there is a relatively equal force resisting motion. For instance, in the human body itself, each muscle is paired with a similar one which is designed to counterbalance or resist its action. Thus every physical motion comes from the greater strength and compulsion of one muscle, offsetting the resistance of its opposing twin.

Parenthetically, your job as a supervisor often is one of helping subordinates to gain the added impulse and compulsion it takes to overcome similar resistance and inertia. You probably refer to it as "getting an employee off dead-center." And it is something which you are particularly conscious of doing on Monday mornings and Friday afternoons.

What You Must Know — and Reflect

Clearly, the supervisor must first know his job: its responsibilities and its restrictions, its authorities and its limitations. He must also know himself, and assure that he adapts himself to fulfill the needs of the job and the normal job expectancies of those who work under his jurisdiction. Finally, he must clarify for those with whom he works what his responsibilities are: what comprises their scope, and what are their limits.

Orienting a newly appointed supervisor, Joe Holt, a highly respected no-nonsense mill superintendent, emphasized, "When you are totally clear in your own mind what your responsibilities are — and what the limits of your responsibilities are — you understand and can clarify to your subordinates what your working relationships actually involve, and where they stop. Then you never let people down by being unable to give them the support which you might otherwise have led them to expect in an area outside of your capability and responsibility. And, important too, when they know what to expect of you, they equally know what you expect from them — and you get it."

Basic requirements are often briefly and generally summarized as:

1. Know your job.
2. Know yourself.
3. Know the jobs of your subordinates.
4. Know your subordinates.
5. Understand what your people want and need *from* and *in* their jobs.
6. Understand what people want and expect from their supervisor.

The Job of Supervising

Because it is obviously important, we often place too much and too exclusive emphasis on the need for each individual — non-supervisor, supervisor, manager, executive — to know his own job. This, of course, is fundamental: obviously one must know his job in order to do it. But it does not stop there: to be effective, the job of supervision must be known to those who work under its leadership and guidance, as well as to those who actually occupy the job. When you think of all jobs as consisting of team effort and group achievement, it becomes very clear that each supervisor and each worker must go beyond the knowledge requirements of his own job, must understand the work relationship of his efforts, and must clearly see how his personal actions fit to this working relationship.

For instance, an employee must know the responsibilities and authorities of his immediate supervisor — as they pertain to him, and as he relates to them. He obviously must know, too, the succeeding or preceding job or operation, at least insofar as his own job relates to them or is influenced by them. And it is the supervisor's direct responsibility to assure that each worker has such an understanding, not only as it pertains to himself and his own job, but also as it applies to the interrelationship of people and jobs under his jurisdiction.

Explaining his reason for providing supervisory training to non-supervisory people who were not candidates for immediate promotion, Mr. Bramlette McClelland, President of Houston-based McClelland Engineers, explained, "A man must understand what supervision means and consists of — must know its responsibilities and limitations — in order to properly and fully accept and utilize supervision. And, also, a man must know how to *be* supervised before he can learn and prepare to supervise others."

In a New England textile mill, a newly appointed supervisor selected several of the so-called mavericks in his department as members of a work-study group. He outlined for them the specific problems with which he wanted their help, and clarified the supervisory consideration with which he would have to judge and select the appropriate answers. For instance, he mentioned group reaction and interaction, relationships with other departments, scheduling, and work-deployment requirements.

Initial words of introduction are never adequate to attain workable understanding of new approaches, problems, and viewpoints. So the early suggestions of this group had to be thoughtfully and painstakingly analyzed and rejected. But within five or six months, the program achieved the desired results: a number of excellent and workable suggestions were offered by the committee; and the committee members commenced to spread understanding and recognition of supervisory problems and points of consideration among those with whom they most immediately worked.

Knowing Yourself as a Supervisor

But before you can confidently practice your role and responsibilities as supervisor — and thereby reflect to your subordinates what they should or should not expect of you — you must first not only understand the duties themselves, but also be able to visualize yourself in this new relationship with people and how you must adjust to fulfill these requirements. Bluntly, you must understand not only the nature and degree of your required adjustment, but its limits as well.

Certain psychological tests are extremely helpful to a supervisor in setting himself on the right track, and in making this transition effectively. This is not to suggest that a new supervisor should try to change himself; actually, if he tried to do so, he would become inconsistent and insincere. But different kinds of work and occupations have different requirements: the requirements which we meet quite naturally and spontaneously because of our related interests, personality characteristics, or personal tendencies are, in effect, strengths insofar as that occupation is concerned. Requirements which do not match up to our personalities or interest inclinations are weaknesses, insofar as the job is concerned, and need special care and concentration for us to meet the requirements.

For instance, psychological tests show us the extent (great or small) to which we have an interest in the factors that personally influence people. Those who have an extremely high degree of interest in this are inclined to become excessively involved with their people and with the influences which disturb them. Men and women having an extremely low interest tend to be cold or insensitive to their workers unless they consciously develop this people interest. Supervisor-managers who have a significantly low scoring in "persuasiveness" do not, by basic nature, do an effective job in training, developing, or instructing their subordinates. Those with an accompanying high score in "people-interest" are inclined to request once, and then, in the face of non-responsiveness or resistance on the part of the workers, proceed to do the work themselves. Or when "persuasiveness" and "people-interest" scores are both low, the supervisor-manager has a tendency to order, mandate, or demand, rather than instruct, guide, lead, and motivate his people.

To attain creditable performance as supervisors we must know *ourselves,* and know *our jobs,* and then critically examine what needs to be done to put the two together constructively and productively. Psychological tests help in this, and in trying to foresee what our work relationships problems may be, by giving us objectivity to "see ourselves as others see us."

A Change of View and Viewpoint

There is no doubt that the most difficult and disconcerting transition a man or woman ever makes in life is the move from a nonsupervisory job to supervisory responsibility. "Something funny happens," one newly appointed supervisor commented. "All of a sudden you're not part of the bunch anymore. Some of the folks with whom you have been friendly become distant; others seem hostile or suspicious; and some seem more overtly friendly than ever before. Your first tendency is to prove that you are personally unchanged — but this inevitably leads to frustration and trouble, because you find that you are accused of favoritism; or you get deluded into thinking that your personal popularity is the key and you soon find that you thereby lose your effectiveness. Ultimately you must recognize that the usefulness and leadership you provide for your work group, as much as your effectiveness as a management representative, depend on your understanding and acceptance of your altered role and relationships."

In reality, your whole viewpoint must change as you move into the role of supervision. It's sort of like backing away from a workbench where you have been assigned for a long time. You must still see that same occupation clearly and distinctly but now, as a supervisor, you must see it and its importance as they relate to others. You must see both jobs and people in perspective. You must commence to focus on *results,* rather than on the details of how a job is done. You must begin to see people for what they can do, instead of entirely for what they are. And you must recognize that this is what your workers and your bosses alike expect of you.

Observations of many newly appointed supervisors show that the majority at first go to one extreme or the other. They try to fulfill their responsibilities either through overt efforts to be popular with their subordinates, or by exercising authority through demand. Long experience indicates that neither approach works by itself. The popularity of the supervisor must be based on popularity *as* the supervisor. He is judged on his record for fairness, reasonableness, understanding, equitable treatment, perspective, and leadership. This nature of popularity is needed to inspire and to secure the favorable and productive response of people to orders, directions, or instructions issued by a supervisor.

Discipline — and Motivation

Our lives are structured by discipline. In greatest measure, this is discipline which we have accepted, either because it is for our own individual or group well-being, or because it is an essential "rule of the game" for something we elect to do. A great deal of our sense of security and well-being rests in knowing clearly what this discipline consists of, and why it exists. We feel that we are conforming to all that is required of us when we measure up to its clear specifications.

Rules and disciplinary guidelines of course must have understandable purpose, reason, and justification. Too often such company and departmental regulations are obsolete or arbitrary or have not been amended to provide reasonably for employee problems. For instance, a supervisor in Bangkok, where rush-hour problems cause a great deal of morning tardiness, felt that morning signing-in was an arbitrary, unfair, and unnecessary rule. So he passed the sheet around in his department each afternoon for the employee to sign in advance and commented, happily, "I've had no reported lateness or absence in my department in over six months."

But if the rules of the game are sound, equitable, reasonable, and supportable, their discipline often amplifies or enhances the sense of importance or value which the individual obtains from the work itself. Conversely, an athlete who breaks training rules does not merely repudiate the discipline, he also reduces his own valuation of his sport, and of his self-worth as a participant. Very often a large share of the value placed on athletics is the rigorous discipline it requires. The self-esteem of the athlete is gained through his capability to endure the discipline and to achieve its results. Value, difficulty of attainment, and discipline are vital factors of human motivation.

Discipline — and Value

A young paratrooper told me, "The value of life is never clear and distinct until you find something of value for which you would be willing to give up your life. Once you do, you find that discipline is both a part and a reminder of the value of the thing to which you have committed yourself. In my opinion, this is what the so-called generation gap is all about: young people tested parental discipline, partly to find out its reasonableness, rationality, and supportability, and partly to find out the strength and consistency with which their parents believed in the discipline, and valued the goal which the discipline was supposed to support. So when parents responded with permissiveness, young people necessarily interpreted this to mean that the discipline was arbitrary, unreasonable, and unsupportable, and that the objectives and goals were not of important value. It sure didn't leave us with any guidance for our beliefs or values — or with a very favorable outlook regarding the beliefs, values, or guts of our parents."

Resentment, resistance, and dislike, then, are an inherent and inevitable response toward discipline and toward the person or source by which it is represented or enforced. Yet a measure of this — and the gripes by which it is expressed — are healthy and essential. The Marine Corps study of a few years ago showed that a certain measure of griping reflected healthy morale; that silence and apathy were precarious. In one of the happiest, healthiest, and most loving family relationships I know, the two boys refer to their father as "a driver — and a perfectionist"; their mother refers to her husband as "restless and irritating"; and her husband refers to her as "the war department." Collectively and individually, through the discipline they represent and share with each other, this family has attained enviable expertise in several personal and occupational areas.

For the sensitive supervisor who understands his people and tries to fulfill his responsibilities as a leader *for* and *to* his people, gripes can be an eloquent and encouraging language. But to the man who tries to get too close and too personal, who believes that effective supervision depends upon personal popularity, they can be unnerving and destructive.

The two most popular commanding officers under whom I served in the Navy were also, by more than coincidence, the most strict and formal. Commenting on one of them, an officer said, "Sure, the old man's strict: he's all business, and implies that personal relationships are between each other, and not with him. The captain knows his job, he's fair, he's equitable in his treatment of people; I respect him — and I feel that to the extent that I know my job and do it, I will always have his respect, as well. It thereby gives me a feeling of self-respect and reliability. You always know where you stand with him, and these things are particularly vital in this industry."

The other captain once told me, "When you take on a position of command, you exchange a part of your personal license and latitude for its responsibilities. When you are non-supervisory, your responsibility is only one-way, to your boss. But when you become supervisory, your responsibilities are two-way, upward and downward, to your bosses and to those who are under your jurisdiction. It's hard to say which direction is most important, to your bosses or to your subordinates. But one thing is for certain: you will never fulfill your responsibilities to *either* unless you are willing to surrender some of your personal and personality assertions, unless you are willing to reflect that your dedication to your job and to your people outweighs your personal and personality needs. I guess what I'm really saying is that you have to learn to put first things first, and yourself second."

What People Expect of You

If we are to outline what people expect of you, we must commence by enumerating a few of the things which people *want* and *need* in their jobs, their work, and their companies, which are necessarily centered in *you,* and what you represent and provide to them. As we indicated earlier, in our discussion of the job of supervision, you are partly a *person* and largely a *role* or occupational centerpoint to your people. The old cliche that "you represent your company to your subordinates" is more true and more basic than most of us have ever adequately recognized.

In an off-the-record speech to a top management audience, the placement director of one of the country's leading universities commented, "I don't believe that there is any such thing as company loyalty!" The strong debate caused by this statement led the university thereafter to conduct a limited and informal study. Half of the companies selected for research were those in which a high degree of company loyalty was believed to exist; the other half consisted of companies in which the absence of company loyalty was regarded as a key and crucial problem.

The survey upheld the placement director's opinion and did something more; it showed that often the "people reaction" which we had historically called company loyalty in reality was a reflection of a favorable interaction in response between people themselves. Where supervisors at all levels had built sound and responsive interrelations and rapport, the thing which we had been calling company loyalty was strongly evident. Where supervisory interrelationships were less favorable, or were poor, this company loyalty trait did not exist.

In other words, loyalty is most clearly and noticeably a bond between people. What we had for so many years called company loyalty was nothing more or less than the total or aggregate effect of such a "people bond" built by effective and sensitive supervisors, the result of good supervisory practices and relationships.

Some writers and authorities have minimized this by suggesting that it exists merely because the immediate boss represents the company and its management to people under his jurisdiction. But it goes a lot further and deeper than that. Leadership comes from direct interaction: unless it is secured from the supervisor, it does not exist for the work group; so far as job values, assignments, morale, motivation, future prospects, support, understanding are concerned, the supervisor does not merely *represent* the company, he *is* the company to those who are under his jurisdiction.

Whether we call this "company loyalty" or "supervisory human interaction," it is a thing which all companies increasingly need in order to meet the ever-intensifying demand for productivity, progress, innovation, and flexibility. Yet as much as companies need it, work people themselves need it even more. Such affinity is vital and of ever-growing importance to people; all of the increasingly recognized questions of identity, self-worth, fulfillment, motivation, and accomplishment are inseparably tied to the favorability of the supervisor-worker relationship.

What — and How — People Understand

Because we are basically social, one of our strongest and most fundamental compulsions is toward relationship and relating. Many of our human reactions and responses are thus designed either to explore, establish, or to sustain our human relations potentialities and prospects. In effect, we therefore assess all people and places with an underlying question: "How does this [or her, or him] pertain to me?" or "How do I potentially relate to it [or to him, or to her]?" This examination is actually meant to operate in two directions, intending both to determine how a thing or person potentially relates to us, and how we potentially relate to or fit in with every situation or person that we encounter.

Whether we are aware of this, or do it unconsciously, this assessment is a constant and ever-active process. For instance, if you are sitting home in the evening, relaxedly reading your newspaper in the company of your family at the time when the doorbell unexpectedly rings, your assessment of a potential relationship commences even before you move from your chair. You begin to anticipate the potentiality of the pending relationship in terms of the time of evening, and what visits at a similar time of day have meant to you in past experience. As you approach the door, your assessment becomes somewhat directionalized by the environmental circumstances of the pending meeting. Because it is to take place at your home, and during non-work hours, it leads you to thoughts of a social or domestic nature of relationship. As you open the door, your first assessment probably is in terms of the potential or possible dangers of the relationship, and when your protective responses have been satisfied, your assessment then leads you into more general and relaxed tones.

The interpretation — or the meaning which a person derives from an act, expression, or circumstance — depends entirely on how, as an individual, these specific things may have pertained to him, affected him or influenced him. Most noticeably, when a man has had prior experience with fire, it is evident that he is assessing a building which he is entering for the first time in terms of its potential dangers, its escape routes, its flammability, its fire prevention. Not too differently, when a new employee enters a work area for the first time, he assesses its exits, as well as its entrances, and the physical and intangible factors which he "reads" as favorable or unfavorable.

Experience or teaching suggest what an object, sound, or appearance means to us, or implies to us, and how we therefore should respond. For instance, if we were to use our earlier example of the home doorbell ringing at night, we think of the stranger being dressed either in a nun's habit or a black facial mask, we can see that our resulting response of friendliness or fear is based on what we have learned that these two appearances imply to us.

By far the most critical and sensitive appraisal of all is the assessment which a new employee gives to his supervisor. The employee has so much at stake; and the relationship with the supervisor is one in which the individual is entrusting his hopes, aspirations, economic needs, and his physical, mental, and emotional well-being. Thus, in this hyper-tense scrutiny, the new employee searches every word, tone, gesture, act, expression to determine "How do I relate to him?" and "How does he relate to me?"

Your employee is looking to you as his new boss in an effort to understand you and with the expectancy of being understood by you. Your employee draws conclusions both from what he sees, feels, hears, and believes is implied, and from what he expects to hear from his boss.

The Basis for Worker Understanding

What the new man understands and interprets in relying on the guidelines of his own prior experience and learning sometimes, of course, will be erroneous; situations and circumstances may differ in their meaning. But he expects his new boss to recognize and clarify these differences. Also, there are some areas in which he has had no prior experience and teachings to guide him. Somehow he expects his new supervisor to realize these omissions and deficiencies and, without coaching, to explain the meaning and inferences, and how they should be seen and interpreted. The supervisor who *does* recognize and answer these unspoken questions is appraised as an understanding boss and a leader; the one who does *not* is regarded as insensitive and lacking in understanding.

An employee's expectation of leadership and understanding from his supervisor reflects an extremely vital aspect of the responsibility and the importance of supervision. This defines what people expect, want, and need from the boss. If he supplies it, and fulfills their needs, he is a leader and a motivator, and quickly and continuously forms the bond which we previously called company loyalty. If he does not supply it, these essential factors of employee relations remain absent and unfulfilled because no one else is in the strategic position to supply them.

When we realize and accept this, we can also readily understand the multitude and varieties of human work and non-work situations for which an employee will turn to his supervisor as a source of the only accreditable and valid answer. An employee inevitably feels that his supervisor should understand him — and thus will know his skills, potentialities, and how they relate to the occupation and the future of the company. Basically, a worker grows to feel that his supervisor will realize that the question "How does this pertain to me?" constantly arises, whether it is verbalized or not, and that the boss will understand him so well and so completely that he can also recognize and understand the varied personal problems which have influence on his work.

Helping Your People to "Size You Up"

As a West Coast technical supervisor-manager expressed it, "When you accept the fact that supervision is not a popularity contest, and that your subordinates are concerned about the man who occupies your job, rather than the personal you, things get a lot clearer and surer. You are less apt to take things too personally, and to be hurt by them; you know better what is expected of you by both your bosses and your subordinates; and you have a better sense of the needs that you can fulfill by doing your job well. It doesn't minimize your sense of personal value; it merely redirects it more appropriately and makes you feel a sense of the value of your job and your competence in doing it. Most important of all is that it makes you realize what people need from one in your job, that they cannot get or satisfy in any other way, from any other source."

Because similarly experienced supervisors have told me the employee's essential need for "a boss who is understanding," I used a related question in workshop sessions which I conducted throughout the United States, eastern Canada, and three Asian nations. In each workshop, mixed groups from differing industries with varied managerial job titles were chairmanned by a member of their own choosing who thereafter served as a spokesman in presenting a summary of the group's views and conclusions to a large seminar group.

The thoughts and suggestions of these workshop groups were amazingly similar. And I felt that the chairman-spokesman of a Dallas group represented a broad consensus and phrased it well when he said, "The thing that you must remember about building communications is that it cannot be an immediate and spontaneous accomplishment. The kind of communications we're talking about requires confidence, and the building of confidence comes through backing up the words we say with action and attitude. We must be consistent, and people who work for us have got to feel and see the same views and attitudes that they hear in what we say."

Employees *want* and *need* things from their supervisors — personal, occupational, and motivational answers which they cannot get anywhere else. But before they can seek, understand, or accredit them from a supervisor, they must first learn that these things are readily and consistently available. As one supervisor aptly expressed it, "They have got to know us; we have got to communicate with our words, actions, and attitudes. We've got to give them time, as well as opportunity, to know us and to have confidence in us."

In a recent casual chat with a long-service woman employee from a department in which a new supervisor had been assigned to replace a rather unpopular predecessor, I asked offhandedly, "How do you like your new boss?" She answered thoughtfully: "He appears to be a very good choice. He seems to know the work and the job; he seems to like it here, and to have a good general attitude; he seems to have a lot of human understanding. It would be wonderful if he proves out — if he turns out to be what he appears to be."

As an interesting footnote, I found that the supervisor had set up a private "get acquainted" conference with each employee in his department. He started each discussion with the phrase, "Someday I hope that you will have learned to understand me and to trust me. But that's going to take time; I have no right yet to ask or expect your trust. I need to ask you a lot of questions, in order to understand you and the operation. If there are any questions you are hesitant to answer — or feel are just none of my business — just don't answer: okay?"

"Incidentally," he continued, "if there is anything you want to ask me, go ahead and ask it. And if I'm hesitant to answer — or feel it isn't any of your business — I'll just skip it, too." Before his round of conferences was completed, he had not only learned a lot about the people and the operation, but he had also progressed a long way in developing rapport with his people.

What You Said — Versus
What Your Subordinate Hears

Did you ever stop to think how often, when you were a child, you watched your father's facial expression to anticipate what his responses would be? Or how carefully you scrutinized your school teacher's face, to see whether or not you were giving the right answer, or had done well or poorly in an exam? Or how often you've relied on the sound of footsteps that tell you someone is happy, angry, tired, or relaxed?

The fact is that when someone's attitude or reaction is important to you, you look for signs, instead of either waiting for words or relying entirely on them. The more such a person represents an important influence in your life, environment, comfort, or future prospect, the more you watch for such signs intensely and hyper-sensitively. What married couple, for example, ever ceases to watch for indications of an attitude which will influence the tenor of their relationship? And what worker has ever failed to keep an eye on the boss to denote moods and reactions which will have a helpful or detrimental effect on the environment of work?

Roy Moynahan, a highly intense and well-qualified technician, was appointed manager of a small plant — a new position in which he zealously aspired to succeed. On the first day of his new assignment he walked through the plant with his customary vigor, stopping in various departments, directing questions to production employees without consulting their supervisors.

Returning a few minutes later from the machine shop where he had gone to discuss a problem, a production supervisor saw one of her girl operators leaving the plant, another sitting beside her machine, crying. "It's not what that guy says or what he does," the weeping operator explained. "It's the way he walks, the way he stands and glares. The way he pounds his heels when he walks and approaches a person is like a swooping vulture — then he just stands there and glares, without saying anything. He makes you feel as if you were doing everything wrong, and the first thing you know, you're all thumbs. I'm quitting."

Confronted by the irate supervisor, Roy Moynahan lamely explained, "But I was just studying the operation, trying to understand it." He hadn't yet recognized that actions speak louder than words, and that a boss is the fundamental symbol of the environment of work.

Sooner or later, every supervisor learns that communications go far beyond words which are planned, programmed, and said. Actually —

1. Ten percent or less of our communication is by words, or "verbal": every human being communicates in some way or to some degree every moment of every day.

2. What we communicate is not necessarily what we intend. The understanding which people receive from our communications depends primarily on how people themselves interpret them. (And our communications responsibilities are not merely to reflect or verbalize what we mean, but instead to make sure that what we mean is understood.)

3. The absence of any clear and comprehensible communication is, in itself, a form of communication. Silence may be oppositely interpreted by workers to be an affirmation that all is well, or that the boss is displeased: it may coincidentally mean to a self-confident worker that he has done a good job, and to an insecure worker that he has "pulled a booboo."

4. To the sensitive employee, every factor and physical aspect of the environment of work can be a message, implication, or communication.

How You Communicate Without Words

In dealing with our friends, we become more relaxed and less conscious of our need to communicate. We say that they "understand" — and that their understanding enables them to go beyond words, beyond the requirement of verbally communicating. The fact is that this is a totally false assumption: actually, our friendship with people enables them to know us better, to know and correctly interpret our feelings and reactions; they know the *meaning* of our responses and are thereby able to receive and interpret communications from our reactions, instead of depending upon words for expression. Friends know us in terms of ourselves — and thus find our actions, and gestures, as well as our words, clearly expressive.

Whether we are conscious of it or not, we learn to rely on nonverbal communication in our relationship with friends. For this reason, with our friends we feel a sense of companionship and constant communication. We get to know them so well that we are able to understand their moods, responses, and feelings through watching their facial expressions, their physical actions, and the way that they walk or stand. In a sense, we recognize that every act, movement, and mannerism becomes a form of communication which is often far more expressive than our words. It is truly too bad that we are not consciously aware of this degree to which we study and interpret the actions of our friends and acquaintances. Because if we were, we would also recognize the fact that every act and expression speaks for us, that truly our "actions speak louder than words." Because actions do speak for us, we are communicating all the time, with and by everything that we do: communication is continuous and constant. In not recognizing the extent to which we communicate non-verbally in our friendly relationships, we fail also to recognize the multitude of ways in which we communicate that we are not then aware of. And we are unaware, too, of how our actions and mannerisms affirm or deny our words.

Shortly after a friend of mine became blind, I visited and found her fully relaxed about discussing her experiences with her new disability. "One of the first things I learned is the extent to which we normally rely on our eyesight in receiving communications," she commented. "Both speaker and listener learn to depend so much on facial expressions to denote emphasis, feeling, and sensitivity, that vocal tones become neglected. It's funny, but now that I can no longer see but must rely entirely on hearing, I detect tones of insincerity in acquaintances and television personalities whom I used to regard as totally sincere."

The *meanings* derived from our communications being understood by people who do not know us personally are not necessarily in terms of what we *mean* to communicate. The interpretations given to our verbal and non-verbal communications by someone who does not know us well are not based on his interpretation of *us*. Instead, they are based on what the person himself would mean by such responses, actions, or words, *or* on what he may have learned in other relationships that these communications imply to him, personally and individually.

How You Can Communicate Non-Verbally

Several years ago a traditionally profitable company was confronted with deficit figures in its operation. Investigation revealed that this was due to product-line breaks, slow repairs, down-time. An audit showed that the most severe experience was within the 45-minute period from 8:30 until 9:15 in the morning. Further exploration reflected that this was the exact timing of the daily plant-tour of the operating vice president.

Vance Normand, the vice president, was generally regarded as a technical genius; he had invented many of the machines then operating in the plant. He was also well-known for his capacity for intense concentration, in which he became virtually unaware of his surroundings. People who knew him personally were very fond of him, and regarded him as a gentle and thoughtful person. But, of course, people more remote from him were somewhat awed by his austere title.

Mr. Normand's habitual routine was a 15-minute visit with the president at the start of the morning to discuss and plan operational matters. Thereafter, he made his daily plant-tour, enroute to his office. Unfortunately, at this time Mr. Normand's head was filled with technical matters and he walked through the plant in a virtual haze of concentration. Because of this preoccupation, his answers to greetings from employees seemed to be more a growl than a voice, and his apparently hostile outlook scared people; after all, he was "the boss."

The result was that people hid, as best they could, as they saw him approach. The lucky ones suddenly took their coffee-breaks or smoke-breaks, or visited the medical department for check-ups. The not-so-lucky ones merely became extremely busy on the opposite sides of the machines they operated.

Unknowingly and unintentionally, this man upset the morale of a thousand workers on his daily tours because he non-verbally and inaccurately communicated hostility and displeasure. This is not what he meant, and it was not the kind of a guy he was. But this is what workers saw and interpreted. And communications are based on what they mean to recipients, not what is meant by the sender. Mr. Normand's non-verbal communication was eloquently erroneous.

The effective supervisor fully capitalizes the power of non-verbal communication — but uses it in a *positive* sense. As insurance against being misunderstood through a possible lack of clarity and explanation, he uses every positive non-verbal symbol — smiles, responses, appearances of favorable attitudes — to reassure his workers and project to them a sense of security, friendliness, understanding, and interest.

Understand Your "Place" — and Keep It

Responsibility to and for people demands that we sensitively understand people in terms of themselves, their feelings, and their problems — but that we retain perspective. In other words, professions and jobs with "people responsibilities" demand that we be empathetic and maintain perspective. We inevitably lose this with too-close and too-sympathetic personal involvement.

One of the most crucial lessons a supervisor learns — often rather painfully — is that subordinates expect and need a boss to act consistently in his role as a supervisor. Workers expect a supervisor to keep his place, and to retain perspective at all times. Personal involvement is even more of a disservice to workers than it is to company management, and any act of involvement is regarded by workers as an indication of favoritism, subjectivity, and undependability. Involvement also leads inevitably to personal hurt feelings for the supervisor.

After one of my early union contract negotiations — one in which I felt that I had been abusively treated — I sought out the chairman of the union's negotiating committee and asked him, "Is this the way you guys really feel about me — and toward me?" He looked at me somewhat amusedly and said, "Of course not, you knuckleheaded numbskull; don't take things entirely on their superficial appearances — this is just negotiations and negotiating tactics. The guys like you well enough — and what's a great deal more important, they respect you, and regard you as fair."

Overhearing the conversation, the thoughtful union president took me aside and counseled, "What you've got to learn, if you're going to be an effective manager or executive, is *don't take things too personally*. And that works *both* ways: don't let yourself become too personally involved with people, and don't expect too much personal consideration from them. Remember, work is not a popularity contest — people aren't working here because they like you; they're working here because it's their job, because they want to work here, and because they're getting paid for it. If you get too personally involved with them, they'll feel that you're not doing your job fairly and objectively. If you expect too much of them personally, you're going to be let down, disappointed, and hurt."

5

BUILDING THE BRIDGES OF
YOUR WORKING RELATIONSHIPS

"It's unbelievably hard to get an answer in this company," one worker complained. "If you go to the boss with one simple question, 20 minutes later you are still standing there, hearing him talk all around the question but never answering it. When it's all over, you leave without getting the answer. All I want is a simple *yes* or *no,* or a promise that he will look into the question and consider it.

"The result is that all of the boys have concluded that the boss is terribly insecure, and that he either doesn't know how to make a decision, or is afraid to do so. We feel that he's insecure because of the way he uses any and every question to show how much he knows on the subject, and because if he weren't *afraid* to make a decision, he'd go ahead and do it, and save all of us a lot of time."

Recognize Why You Need to Communicate

Whether or not we consciously realize it (or admit it, even to ourselves), we are often inclined to let self-purposes intrude in our communicating. Thus, not all of our actual objectives are appropriate or effective, either in transmitting information or in achieving desired communications results. Examining communications candidly and critically, we recognize that the objectives may be:

1. to express ourselves,
2. to be personally understood (or appreciated),
3. to relate ourselves to others,
4. to relate others to ourselves,

5. to affirm or reassure ourselves by verbalizing our knowledge, fittedness, or value,
6. to placate or quiet a problem — get listener quiescence or satisfaction (rather than understanding),
7. to answer questions — or to dispense new information,
8. to secure understanding of thoughts and ideas,
9. to build mutuality of understanding,
10. to build relationships.

Because the first six of these possible objectives are so obviously out of tune with tasteful and effective communications, we rarely follow such courses intentionally. But, more often than we realize, we conduct our communicating in just such manner.

Similarly, the young and newly appointed general manager of a 200-employee manufacturing plant in Connecticut developed an early practice of holding 45-minute Monday-morning meetings with the department heads for which he announced no agenda but in which he delivered carefully prepared monologues.

Supervisory people complained: "These are on-the-carpet sessions"; "No one is given a chance to give reasons or explanations"; and "They're a rehash of what's gone wrong."

The general manager's actual purpose of proving himself to his subordinates backfired. As the plant superintendent remarked, "When a guy tries to show how much he knows, he usually ends up doing just the opposite. We wouldn't normally expect a guy in his job to know all the answers. But when he holds himself up as an all-inclusive authority, he's actually competing with us rather than working with us. So we have become critical, are more aware of what he obviously doesn't know than what he's trying to demonstrate that he *does* know."

Conference Communications Can Help — Immensely

When thoughtfully planned, group meetings can help a great deal in building the bridges of working relationships *with* your people and *between* your people simultaneously, as design and drafting manager John Connally demonstrated. John was faced with the difficult situation of being hired from the outside and over the heads of all the aspiring people within a large and diverse department. He immediately found that the department was fractionalized by internal jealousies, frictions, and lack of cooperation. And despite a strong pre-employment assurance that no one in the department was eligible or qualified for promotion into the job, John discovered two long-service employees who he felt were better qualified for the job than he was.

John immediately scheduled a program of private interviews with each employee of the department. These were described in advance as get-acquainted discussions, to familiarize himself with the people, organization, and operation, and to let them know whatever they wanted to know about him and about his plans. During these discussions, he told them of a meeting program that he would be instituting, outlined his purposes and expected agenda, and asked for suggestions as to what should be included.

In his discussions with key people, he appointed them as members of the discussion group, and assigned them individual topics about which he specifically wanted them to talk. He made it clear that group discussion would be limited to facts which pertained to the group as a whole, that topics relating specifically and exclusively to single units of the department, or restricted to two or three units or their work relationship, were strictly out of order.

Limiting himself to five minutes of presentation, and the weekly sessions to 30 minutes, John chairmanned the first three meetings. Thereafter, he alternated the chairmanship between the two men in the department who he felt were so highly qualified. His own point of emphasis was chiefly his thoughts about departmental relationships and interrelationships, and brief announcements of pending new plans and programs. He made himself accessible to questions, which he either answered directly or provided answers for at the next session.

John pointedly and rather brusquely stifled all bickering in the meetings, but followed up immediately to see what he could personally do to resolve the problems. Agendas of the meetings were constructed from problems or questions that arose during meeting intervals and were supplemented by subjects developed or introduced in the course of the sessions.

At the end of six months, John assigned the two co-chairmen entire responsibility for the agenda and conduct of meetings, and increasingly he "was busy elsewhere" during the sessions, except when he was specifically asked to attend. A year later, when John announced to the operations vice-president that the two co-chairmen were "qualified, capable, and ready" to take his job, and simultaneously submitted his own resignation, he was appointed plant manager because, as the vice-president indicated, "We need throughout the plant exactly the kind of relationships, interest, and productive harmony you have built so quickly and effectively in this one department."

Underneath it all, John Connally had in large measure what the young general manager most specifically lacked — self-confidence, and thereby a sense of self-security. These are battles which we must fight privately within ourselves, and which we cannot expect jobs, position, or authority to solve for us.

How Our Self Needs Distort Us

Insecurity within ourselves leads us to be excessively critical of ourselves — and of those for whose work we are responsible. In the face of feelings of insufficiency in any aspect of ourselves, or our jobs, or our knowledge, we tend to magnify our inadequacies out of all due proportion until we lose perspective on ourselves, our jobs, and the reactions and performance of others. It becomes impossible for us to view ourselves, our work, and our responsibilities objectively — to properly assess the relative importance of the various factors and details. We are too insecure to take chances. Thus we become perfectionists, ignoring the normal fallibility in the thoughts, actions, and efforts of human beings; we leave no reasonable latitude for errors, either in ourselves or in those with whom we work and live. We become critical because we are fearful.

Show me a guy whom people call "an extreme perfectionist" and most often he will be a man who is so terribly unsure of himself that he picks very limited, restricted, "safe" standards to which he himself conforms — and in which he demands precise conformities from others. It takes a great deal of self-assurance and confident knowledge of jobs and people for a supervisor to give employees the latitude to fully use their own skills, ideas, and methods. As strange as it seems, it takes self-confidence and courage for a supervisor to give commendation and support for achievement, because when you commend a man you defer to his skill and accomplishment. To the extent that it encourages him to greater latitude with his skills and efforts, it reduces your tight control of his activities. But it opens up the door to the development and exercise of your people potential.

Assert Your People — Not Yourself

Dick Randall was badly shaken when his boss retired and a new man was brought in from the outside to fill the vacancy. Dick had won extreme personal respect by overcoming insurmountable personal odds. Restored by sheer determination and guts from broken health caused by Nazi P.O.W. confinement, Dick next contracted poliomyelitis and became crippled from the waist down.

"There isn't another guy in ten million who could get over that, either physically or emotionally. But Dick did — by guts, determination, and ruthless driving of himself," a foreman commented. "There's the whole key to the problem of Dick: he got there by driving himself ruthlessly. Although he doesn't need it anymore, ruthless driving has become his way of life, both in the way he treats himself, and the way he treats other people as well. If he could just get over the hump and relax, he'd be a wonderful boss — but as it is now, people fear him and dislike him."

Dick resigned his job, relocated in a distant part of the country, and spent several months in planned recreation and study. During this time, he followed activities designed to make him realize that he had fully accomplished what he had needed to do in self-restoration. With this his sense of self-security became restored, and his relentless driving and excessive criticalness of himself and others became relaxed.

His next job was a plant superintendency, from which he rose in two years to become executive vice president of his new company. During the emergency of his health situation, Dick had necessarily concentrated solely on himself and on his own goals. It was his success in this that enabled Dick to rejoin the world of other people.

Now that he was ready to be included in the activities and goals of other people, he had to adjust to including them in his, as well. Once he had ceased to be self-assertive, he had quickly won the reputation for communicating understanding and appreciation of people. Now his own experience of pain, suffering, and struggle became a positive thing, rather than a negative one, because it made him able to understand these things in other people. His success in his job as superintendent had been because of the support which he inspired from people with whom he worked.

Very simply, the job of supervision is to activate and press forward people and their aptitudes constructively and productively. So it is very clear that the man who tries — or needs — to assert *himself* can never do an effective job of supervision.

Stop, Look, and Listen

As part of the agenda of a seminar which I conducted in 24 areas of the United States, Canada, and three Asian nations, small groups of supervisors from different companies and varied industries were asked to discuss the question, "How can I be sure that I am hearing all that my employees are saying — or need to say?"

Although they proposed a wide variety of communications techniques which they had individually found effective, their more generalized suggestions were:

1. Know your people.
2. Listen with your eyes; watch for variations in acts and expressions of your people.
3. Ask questions — general and specific.
4. Use new information as a sounding board for exploring the individual employee's need to communicate.
5. Always have time — and present the opportunity to communicate.
6. Establish routines, so that each employee will be contacted for individual conversation at fairly frequent intervals.
7. Watch changes in productivity, absenteeism, turn-over, tardiness — and find out *why*.
8. Note changes in the length of time people take for smoke-breaks, luncheon-breaks, and coffee-breaks.
9. Test out non-personal subjects and communications you receive from vocal employees by questioning workers who are more reluctant to talk.
10. Be sure that you set the example of adequately communicating.

The spokesman for one group suggested that, from his own experience, "I feel that the answer to communicating — like the answer to work — is in getting employees to participate. My experience has been that if you continuously ask questions, and seek for opinions and ideas from your people, you make them feel that they are participating in the operation of the department. Then when problems arise, you find that they communicate readily and easily. What I'm saying, I guess, is that you've got to build a communications habit, both in yourself and in your workers. If you're consistent with communicating and seeking communications, you build a pipeline which employees use whenever they have something special to say or to ask."

Is Your Communication Two-Way — or Four-Letter?

Shortly after the superintendent of a plant had been transferred because of complaints that he had used profane and obscene language in his communications with women employees, I made a scheduled visit of several hours in the plant. As I walked about, observing operations, I became extremely aware of a high-pitched conversation among three or four women workers. The obscenities which each was using were about as crude and vulgar as any I have ever heard.

So I walked over to the area in which the women were working, and commented, "I'm a little confused. Just a few days ago you demanded that your boss get canned because he used profane language. But your language would make his sound like a church litany. What gives?"

The woman who seemed to be the loudest and most proficient in the off-color language immediately spoke up, "Look, that's something else entirely. Between ourselves, it's just talking; it's impersonal. But when the boss uses profanity, that's personal. Furthermore, it's demeaning, because when the boss uses it it reflects an attitude of disrespect. It's a funny thing; we swear among ourselves, but none of us has ever used profanity in talking to a boss. Guess it's because of the difference in the relationship. A boss should never use bad language — no matter what. Especially, a male boss should never use profanity in speaking to female employees."

More as an incident than by formal observation, I have generally noticed that supervisors — men and women with direct people responsibility — rarely use profanity or obscenity. Once I listened with considerable respect and envy as Bill O'Leary, a tall, volatile looking red-headed supervisor, demonstrated remarkable patience and self-control in the face of an obscene verbal onslaught by one of his women subordinates. Bill stood very still; his neck reddened, but otherwise he showed no signs of reaction. As general foreman of an electronics department, Bill, a former merchant seaman, headed a group of 55 women operators and assemblers and 17 male technicians.

Noting the intentness with which I was watching the episode, one of the women operators said to me, "Bless him, Bill never loses his cool. Some of the girls really make a point of bugging him, but they're never able to push him over the brink. He never swears, never shouts; he acts as if he thought we were all ladies, and treats us accordingly. The result is that this is the way he makes us feel and act, toward him and generally toward each other, too. You've really got to admire a guy like that. Even the ones who intentionally bug him have great respect for him."

Just as patience, restraint, and self-control are the marks of a good supervisor, on occasion the use of profanity reflects a serious personality problem on the part of a supervisory manager or executive.

I was once retained by a company to discover the reasons for low productivity and morale among women machine operators and packers. Here it was found that the women workers were resentful about the profane and obscene language used toward them by a company operations officer. Investigation later proved that the man had a deep-rooted psychiatric problem which vented itself toward women.

One of the ladies in the company suggested, "The relationship of boss and subordinate must be one of mutual respect and must be retained on that level. Whatever we are, whatever we do, we seek respect in our work — respect for ourselves first, respect for our work second. And when that respect is lacking, or when it isn't clearly evident, there is bound to be trouble."

Bill Makosky, a naval officer for whose humanness and understanding I have long had high respect, once commented summarily: "Profanity, like joke-telling, is a pretty tricky business. First, to avoid hurting or antagonizing people, you have got to be sure of their receptivity, and even more sure that you are unquestionably impersonal in what you say and the way you say it. As you know, when you're telling what you regard as a funny story, you've got to be pretty sure that the humor and attitude of the listener are very similar to your own. But even more important than that, humor and profanity tie very closely to the basic values and experiences of people; you never can be quite sure when you will offend their values or remind them of an unpleasant or offensive experience."

As a chairman of a seminar work study group reported the consensus of his group members: "The whole purpose of communication is to build understanding and responsive relationship. Since managerial experience indicates that profanity can do little to achieve the communications goal — and most often will do much to destroy it — it seems that wisdom and common sense dictate that profanity be carefully avoided."

Is Communication Really Two-Way?

The fact that opportunity is given for responsive communication, or, for that matter, that discussion takes place, does not necessarily reflect that communication is truly and adequately two-way. As a matter of fact, the superficially two-way appearance of communication, which discussion gives to group meetings, often leads people to erroneously assume that rapport and mutual understanding have been satisfactorily achieved.

Early in my practice as a management counselor, I was assigned to study and make suggestions regarding a company's internal communications and its administrative need in industrial relations. An exploration of this nature requires complete objectivity and, thus, candor with regard to managerial practices which people feel are inappropriate or inadequate. So I was somewhat upset when mill manager Ted Grimes insisted on introducing me and explaining the survey to groups of foremen and supervisors before he would permit study to commence. His remarks were brief: after telling the group a little about me and about the work which I would be doing, he said, "King will ask you a lot of questions and I wish you would answer him frankly. He's not going to tell us who said what, or even report individual answers, and his work will help the company and help me if you tell him what you really think and feel."

The candor of the comments by employees and foremen and the frequently repeated remark, "Okay, well, Ted said to tell you everything," made me recognize that my initial misgivings were virtually groundless. One foreman, who had been absent at the time of the introductory meeting, refused to talk to me until he had checked with Ted. But after he had done so, his thoughtfully frank comment expertly summarized the basic communications problem. "The only trouble with Ted," he remarked, "is that he's just one guy — and there are 4800 of us in the plant. Ted is well liked, and is a highly respected boss. People here would do anything for that guy, and he seems to have an intuitive sense about what people need, and what they need to know. But even if you are able to 'best-guess' all of that, instinctively know what people need, they still have a need to express themselves, and one set of ears is just not enough to fill the needs of 4800 people; it's not possible to be that accessible. What Ted needs to do is to hire extra sets of ears, just as he did you. He should tell us that they are ears we can trust, as we trust him, and that the extra ears will be accessible to us, and will have complete and continuous access to him."

The point was well taken; while it is essential both to a company and to its workers that employees' thoughts, responses, attitudes, and needs be known, workers have a vital need to feel that they are expressing themselves, that communication is two-way and that they are participating in it. This is like the vital importance of feeling that a boss is "accessible": workers may not know *why* or *how* they may want this; in fact they may never have reason to utilize the accessibility of the supervisor-manager. But to know that this is

always available somehow gives them a sense of security, participation, and individual identity and well-being. It becomes a favorable part of the "environment" of work.

You Must Activate Communications

But mere accessibility and availability are not enough. Supervisors
must continuously take the initiative in seeking answers and detect-
ing unfulfilled worker needs *for* communication and *to* communicate. This is partly to reflect the value which the boss places on the
thoughts, ideas, responses, and needs of his work people. And it is
partly to assure that the communications he receives are comprehensively representative. In the average work force only four in
every ten workers express themselves readily, verbalize fluently and
easily; six in ten are more hesitant to express themselves, some to
the point of extreme reticence. The corporation chairman who suggested that he was "well in touch" with his company's employees
because he received frequent notes from varied sources at different
company locations, was seriously in error. Such communication is
by no means representative — it comes from only a few; it's not
comprehensive, since it neglects the range and breadth of employee
interest and need for understanding; and, in general, it is totally
negative.

Just being there is not enough. You must exercise initiative in establishing and maintaining communications with your people.
Initiative is your indication of your interest, and it is vitally necessary to make accessibility meaningful and representative.

These are the reasons why polls of employee opinion are used.
They take the initiative in seeking communications from employees;
they put communications on a basis available and suited to the
communication needs and capacities of all workers; and they secure
total participation and representative conclusions. Unlike other
forms of communication — for instance, mere "accessibility" —
such polls do not depend on the verbal abilities of workers. You
don't hear only the more extroverted workers.

Experience in employee opinion polling showed us the immense
value of the sense of participation and identification which workers
secure from their direct personal involvement. It also reflects the
extreme to which workers respond favorably to the value given by
management to their opinions if they subsequently see their thoughts
being deferred to in management action, policy, and program. To an

increasing degree, opinion polls are followed up with statistical reports and commentaries to employees — and identification of programs and activities which have been adopted as the result of employees' ideas and suggestions expressed in the poll.

A Well-Supervised Program Is Not Enough

The effectiveness of the two-way aspect of communication should be carefully appraised, in even our more modern and updated communications concepts and programs. In a New York State company, in which friendly and spontaneous two-way communications was believed to exist, morale was found to be extremely low — because of poor communications.

Both in meetings and individually, employees were invited to ask questions, make suggestions, and raise comments about the company's operations. "But whenever we do, we find that management takes a defensive stance; instead of regarding such questions as requests for information, they assume that they are criticisms for which they must give excuses," a foreman remarked. "When you ask questions, management seems to feel that this is a criticism. Current business conditions are adverse; they feel insecure, have an intense need to be right. They are defensive about all their actions and decisions — and each time you ask a question, you end up being told why they are *right,* and that something that you have done is *wrong!* All of us have had so many unhappy experiences whenever we've asked questions that we restrict our comments to trivial and non-debatable topics, never daring to communicate our actual thoughts, comments, or occupational needs."

The solution to the communications problem in this company was the appointment of a six-employee "think tank" group, with twice-annual rotation of membership. The chairman of the group was made spokesman, serving as the communications link to management for suggestions generated or developed in the group. Comments made during group discussions remained totally anonymous, were reported only as "committee thoughts and recommendations" — and the group considered questions raised by management and workers, as well as formulating their own ideas. Management developed a policy of answering suggestions at the next meeting subsequent to the one in which the recommendations had developed.

There is widespread and growing concern for communication — and belief that it should be two-way, and supported by active communication-seeking on the part of the supervisory managers. However, you must exercise care to assure that you are always sensitive and give favorable reactions to employee communication. Whenever you solicit ideas and opinions, make sure that they are thoughtfully considered, and are used, wherever possible.

Although it is important to build and sustain two-way communication, inadequate communication is far less detrimental to you than the employees' reactions you will incite through defensive response, lack of constructive reaction, or failure to consider or use the thoughts and opinions you have solicited.

Participation — the Most Penetrating Form of Interaction

"You must be extremely sure of yourself, or very flexible, to do an effective job of communicating," Leo Murphy, Management Consultant, once remarked. "If you merely know the basic subject, and are not experienced with the alternatives — or their possible effects and results — you become very rigid, limiting communications to those narrow areas in which you are sure of your ground. It's only when you have broad knowledge and experience that you're able to relax, be flexible — comfortable in the feeling that you can convincingly cope with side issues."

"People will always make mistakes; this is part of being human," suggested James N. Byers, President of Microfin Corporation. "It's true that one must try to be as accurate as possible. And, with experience, we should learn to be more accurate, to make progressively fewer and fewer errors. But beyond that, the point is that we must not get so tied up by fears of error that we limit our effectiveness and accomplishment — restrict the areas of our potential successes and our learning. Everyone is bound to make mistakes, and you must leave sensible latitude for this in yourself, as well as in others."

The important thing about mistakes is to learn by them — and to avoid repeating them. True, you must face them, accept them, understand them. The supervisor who fails to face his errors never either resolves them or learns by them, and inevitably ends up building them up out of all due proportion. He loses some of the respect of his co-workers and subordinates, although rarely to the degree which he himself ultimately imagines. In the long run, he becomes mistake-prone, more concerned about the possibility of error than the prospect of accomplishment. In other words, he becomes a *negative* supervisor-manager.

Achieving and Accenting Positive Attitudes

Still further, the supervisor who is fearful of making mistakes himself inevitably is the one who fails to delegate. He demands strict adherence to methods and techniques about which he feels secure, and gives his subordinates no latitude to experiment with alternative methods.

To avoid this trap, the supervisor should:

a) Totally familiarize himself with his operation and with its potential productive yield.

b) Note the relative productive yield of his most qualified and motivated worker, and that of his least qualified and motivated worker.

c) Regard this differential as the margin he can provide by training and motivating his workers, by delegating and allowing latitude for the exercise of employee skills and ideas.

d) Compare the "cost" of mistakes and errors with the added productive yield when tight controls and conformity demands have been replaced with interest and motivation.

e) Study specifically the major dangers of the operation — those which can cause emergencies, catastrophes, or major and irreplaceable losses.

f) Devise preventive guidelines and work rules, and communicate these and their reasons to all workers to whom they pertain.

g) Examine all mistakes and errors — your own and those of your subordinates — in terms of the total operation and its accomplishments.

However, these guidelines are meant only to suggest practical measures for securing and retaining the perspective which is essential to effectiveness and positivism in management. Protectionism and tight control drag down productive effort and accomplishment: progress, growth, and development all are founded entirely and exclusively on positive attitudes and outlook. There also are specific guides for building positive attitudes into supervisors' areas of responsibility — and for securing maximum benefits, once these have been attained. No matter how favorably or critically we may otherwise regard them, there are some truly worthwhile and vitally basic objectives in many of the current programs of group dynamics, brainstorming, think-tanks, sensitivity training, and confrontation sessions. These are to:

1. Highlight and remove conditions which serve as restraints to communication by individuals and groups of workers;

2. Offset or counteract verbal hesitancies or inadequacies of individual group members;

    3. Stimulate individual participation; and, thereby,

    4. Achieve group interaction.

As a first step in reducing individual or group hesitancies, all misgivings about embarrassment, backlash, or adverse circumstances must be clearly and unmistakably eliminated. Individuals within the group must become completely reassured that whatever they say in group sessions will remain anonymous, that they will not be judged or held accountable outside the group for any of their acts, comments, or criticism, and that they will not be judged or ridiculed for what they say or the way they express their ideas within the group sessions. Because one major object of working together is to create composite conclusions or recommendations, the responsibility of the individual becomes clearly one of contributing to the group. This involvement stimulates and fulfills workers' motivational need for a sense of belonging and purpose, and the actively contributing member progressively secures a sense of self-worth, value, and accomplishment.

Door Open to New Potentialities

Participating employees develop a broader awareness and understanding of operations and problems. But even more important, they progressively improve their capacity to communicate clearly and to think clearly.

Despite the many valid criticisms of the programs and techniques themselves, their success demonstrates all the more the basic and increasingly vital need of people to secure a sense of self-worth and participation in their work and work relationships. Effective two-way communication assists and retains this sense of self-worth, identification, and participation: one-way communication — or communication which is only superficially two-way — discourages and stifles it.

Exercising Participation and Interrelationship

Two-way communication demands an open mind, as well as an open ear, on the part of the supervisor-manager. You must understand, consider, and act, as well as listen. As in the conducting of group dynamics, the possibility of accountability, or adverse reaction, or misunderstanding, or neglect, all must be clearly eliminated. A supervisor must be receptive to communications, and to the thoughts, motivations, and ideas they transmit.

Communication and interaction are basically like training techniques, which for many years have demonstrated that people need to participate in order to learn and understand. For instance, beyond the point of discussion and demonstration, a time is rather soon reached in training at which it becomes necessary for the trainee to try it for himself, to participate, and to *do*. Similarly now, as job and work-relationships are attaining new levels of recognized importance, it becomes necessary for employees to participate in order to learn and to understand their relationships with their work, their responsibilities, their supervisors, and their co-workers. However, once the sense of participation has been achieved, the worker's interest and response become flexible and progressive — as, equally, does mutual understanding. And people continue to be stimulated by each other — and so work-relationships with other employees, as well as with the supervisor, have progressively favorable and dynamic effects.

The training and motivational value of participation is by no means limited to any one type or level of occupation. And there is virtually no occupation or occupational situation in which the need for understanding is not intensifying as industry updates and progresses — understanding which can be developed *only* through *doing* and participating.

However, communications and participation are extremely sensitive to the environment of work — and can be turned off so readily. There are eight useful guidelines which a supervisor-manager will find helpful in assessing the prospect of favorably helpful interaction with and between his subordinates. These are:

1. Be sure that you provide physical exposure to questions, comments, and suggestions at frequent intervals — both in the employee's work area, and in your own office.
2. Utilize occupational, department, and company subjects with which the employee is familiar to stimulate discussion, and frame these, wherever possible, as questions in order to stimulate ideas.
3. Invite and stimulate questions and comments.
4. Regard questions and suggestions as constructive and well-intentioned, no matter how poor or superficially critical they may appear to be in their phrasing.
5. Consider and objectively evaluate all ideas and alternatives which are offered.
6. Reply constructively to all comments, criticisms, and suggestions.
7. Share some of your thinking processes with the employee, as you consider his questions or suggestions — particularly as you assess

their possible effect on the department or operation as a whole, in perspective.

8. Utilize suggested alternatives when they are feasible and present the potential for constructive or improved results.

And, as with suggestions systems, the opportunity for participation must be uniform and consistent, once it has been established. "Knowing what to expect is extremely important," a non-supervisory worker suggested. The average worker seeks, above all else, an equitableness and consistency in a supervisor's practices and attitudes. And when these have been established in his mind through experience and observation, they become the guidelines of his work responses and actions.

Participation — and Flexibility

Communications — and especially questions, comments, and suggestions — tie in closely to the sensitivities of employees and, thereby, to their subsequent responses. As is true in a number of cases cited by behaviorists, favorable reaction to positive acts or comments stimulates similar future response; negative, hostile, or insensitive reactions are a wet blanket to further comments or questions, and the constructive attitude and interest will be reversed rather than continued.

Most of us recognize how essential receptiveness, responsiveness, and encouragement to constructive attitudes and comments are in building effective communications, mutual understanding, and rapport. They are vital to success in motivating, and "people-building," in even greater degree.

Several years ago, after completing and submitting his questionnaire in an employee opinion poll, a worker sought me out to make additional comments. "I am very glad that this opinion poll is being conducted," he said. "There is something I've had on my chest for a long time and this is actually the first time I've had an opportunity to do something about it." I noted that he had not only completed the questionnaire, but also had written up some comments which he submitted along with it, so it was obvious that whatever it was was quite an issue to him.

"I've worked for this company for 27 years, and conducted my job for all of these years without any complaints from my bosses. Like most guys, sometimes I get a few ideas relating to my job. I don't say too much; however, one time I noticed an oil drip from an overhead bar that was ruining some of the product. Thinking this important enough, I wrote up a suggestion which I passed in to my boss, recommending that a three-inch wide piece of aluminum be bent at a 90-degree angle to form a trough. Hitched at an angle beneath the cross-member, this trough would then catch the oil drip and carry it off harmlessly into a bucket, not affecting the product.

"It wasn't a very important suggestion, but it did have an effect on company profits. Within a week of the time I submitted the suggestion, the trough was put up and the oil drip has never since caused any problem. But nothing was ever said to me. No one ever said it was a good suggestion, or a bad one; no one ever thanked me, or asked for further suggestions. I didn't want any money or recognition for it, but I did feel that the boss or someone else in the company should have said something to me about it — particularly when the idea was immediately put to use. It's bothered me ever since, and this poll is the first chance I've had to sound off about it."

When I asked, "How long ago did this happen?" he answered, "Fifteen years." The old adage, "An elephant never forgets," is a short memory when compared with how people remember an incident which adversely affects their sensitivities, or offends their effort to participate constructively. And when people have once been turned off, it's a major job to get them turned on again.

For a very similar reason, I once selected a militantly negative employee as a member of a work study committee. If this man could be convinced through the familiarity and understanding he would gain by participating in this committee, I would feel more assured that the program, confronted with his criticism on a step-by-step basis, would inevitably be sounder and more workable.

The man turned out to be valuable, sensitive, responsive, and by far the greatest contributor of ideas and excellent suggestions. Visiting a committee session several weeks after it had got underway, the company president adressed the man in front of the whole committee: "Tony, I've known you for 20 years and I've never known you to be so constructive, or realized that you had so many good, practical, and sensitive ideas!"

"I'd like to say that it is just because you haven't looked, George," Tony replied. "But this would be only part of the truth. I'm the same guy, but in this committee, I'm a participant. Undoubtedly my comments and suggestions in the committee are better than the ones I've made throughout the years — but this is because they are based on a better understanding of all the facts and issues; I've learned things by participating. When I come up with something that's not sound, the committee still lets me know it very quickly. It's different, though, because I learn *why* the ideas aren't workable or acceptable, instead of just being ignored or turned off. You know, it's funny — it's much easier for a guy to accept the fact that he's wrong when he's given an opportunity to see *why* he's wrong."

The supervisor-manager who wishes to "control" his subordinates and his work situation will be extremely hesitant to invite participation, just as he similarly will delegate only the routine, "safe," and superficial latitudes of work, judgment, and method.

A few months ago, I conducted an employee opinion poll for a company in which several managers had expressed concern for the number and nature of gripes that had been received. The poll was comprehensive and representative: over 97 percent of the employees fully participated. Ninety-two percent of the participants indicated that they liked their jobs, 89 percent said that they regarded the company as a good place to work, 98 percent commented favorably on their interest in the company and its work, 90 percent commented favorably on the quality of supervision, and 85 to 90 percent reflected their satisfaction by favorable answers to several questions pertaining to the freedom and adequacy of communications.

Gripes are rarely representative; generally they come from fewer than 40 percent of any group of employees. And gripes are not necessarily undesirable. A study made a few years ago of the gripes in the armed services concluded that a certain amount of griping is essential and healthy. It is silence and tension about which a supervisor or an officer must be intently concerned. "It's when it gets quiet that I get worried," one supervisor remarked. "When you see workers getting together in small groups, and talking in low tones — and when the groups break up whenever you pass near them — that's when I feel the twinges in my backbone that tell me there's a problem."

To an increasing degree, supervisor-managers are beoming aware of the importance of the nonverbal communication of their acts, tone, and demeanor. And they are relying, too, on the similar nonverbal communication from which they derive progressive understanding of their workers and their workers' interests and responses.

6

FITTING PEOPLE AND WORK
OBJECTIVES TOGETHER

The key speaker summarized the consensus of a three-day conference of supervisory managers, "The trouble is that there are too
many people in this country who think they can work eight hours
and sleep eight hours in the same eight hours." Commenting on this,
another speaker mentioned an intensive survey of workers which
indicated that 25-30 percent emphatically did not like their jobs.[1]
Let's take an analytical look at what this reflects:

- boredom
- disinterest
- lack of stimulation
- absence of motivation
- lack of work-environment vitality.

Or, summarily, it means lack of effective supervision.

The Supervisor as an "Energizer"

All a company can really buy is a worker's *time*. Like machinery
and equipment, employees' time and their latent skills are the tools
and instruments which the company buys and provides to a supervisor, to utilize in the fulfillment of his job and responsibilities.

Custodianship of these tools and instruments is not enough: these
tools and instruments must all be activated, applied, and productively utilized to mutual benefit. Think for a moment of the matters in

---

[1]Dr. Charles S. Dewey, Professor of Industrial Psychology, Illinois Institute of Technology,
speaking in Minneapolis.

which you have custodial or mere caretaker responsibility, as distinguished from those in which you must provide positive thought, planning, and action. The latter items are those in which you perform and function as a supervisor-manager and clearly indicate your responsibility for worker interest, motivation, stimulation, and the vitality of the departmental work environment.

To do the job you want done, a man has got to put an awful lot of himself into the job. You buy his time — but you additionally need his interests, his efforts, his responsiveness, his understanding. You can acquire and simulate these on a momentary basis, but if your efforts to motivate a worker do not provide for fulfillment of his aims and ambitions, the worker and his interest and responsiveness will soon dry up.

On the one hand, you cannot turn on and fully activate a worker unless you can identify work and performance as the means for fulfilling his motivational needs. But, on the other, if a man conscientiously puts his all into a job in the confident belief that this is the way to attain his goals, he will soon dry up if the job does not give him full return. He will grow to dislike his job, mistrust his supervisor, and become demoralized as to his ability to fulfill his goals and objectives. So if you want a man to put all of these things into his job, you must sensitively concern yourself with what a man can get *out of* his job; if he fulfills the needs of the job, how does the job, in turn, fulfill his needs?

You Must Be Objective

It is essential to attain perspective both on the job and on the aspirations and goals of the worker. For instance: can you sincerely motivate a worker to feel secure and depend on his job and performance, when you know that the job has a definite term, and will become dead-end and obsolete? Can you sincerely assure a worker that the attainment of his aims and well-being will result from dedicated performance when you know either that the promotional or progress potentialities of the work do not measure up to his hopes and expectations, or that those hopes and expectations exceed the realities of his capabilities and potentialities?

Such problems as these are not insurmountable if both the work and worker are viewed with sensitive perspective. If a job is to become obsolete, either the skills or the work reputation an employee gains through performance can be utilized to assure his progress and well-being, when a supervisor plans with perspective. A worker's over-optimistic estimate of his own potentialities can be made more realistic when a supervisor sensitively and candidly assesses the worker's actual prospects, providing guidance in the securing of concrete and feasible aims. And, interestingly, a supervisor can fully motivate a man whose potentialities exceed the prospects of the job and the company if the supervisor both appreciates the value of motivated performance, and understands that "turnover" is not always a dirty word.

In other words, if you truly try to understand your people, it is relatively easy to provide for their motivations when they apply directly to the job, job relationship, or job results. It is somewhat more complex when the motivational value of the job is indirect.

Jim Gaffney, an ambitious and capable young man, illustrates both situations. When he first was hired by an eastern metal-processing company, he liked his work and did it so well that his supervisor suggested that he take outside courses of study which the company would subsidize. For quite some time, this satisfied Jim's motivational needs directly; he was learning in his work, and he was learning in his outside courses, so that in both ways he felt a sense of progress and development. As a result, the supervisor was able to promote Jim and thereby give him a sense of accomplishment.

Finally, after several years and a number of promotions, Jim was reaching the point of becoming over-qualified for any job that the company could offer him, so at this time it became necessary to shift from *direct* motivation to *indirect* motivation. He still wanted to continue his studies, and it was very evident that he had the capacity to learn and progress much further.

So his supervisor called Jim in for a candid chat: "I told him what an excellent job he had been doing for us, that we appreciated him, would hate to lose him. I indicated that I felt that in his own best interests he should continue his studies; that he should stay with us and accept our educational allowances while he worked on the next phase of his studies; that when he completed them, we understood that he would want to find a new job somewhere else and that we would do all that we could to help him find his new place. This is indirect fulfillment of motivation, and some folks have suggested that it is a foolish use of our educational funds. But, believe me, Jim has given us a full return on our investment through his attitude, efforts, interest, and productivity, and it has paid off in the morale of other people, who regard this as a demonstration of our sincere interest in our people."

The whole matter of work and occupational motivation resolves itself into four managerial responsibilities —

1. Understand your people, in terms of their needs and aspirations, and the reality of how these match their capabilities and potentials.
2. Examine jobs, the condition, environment, and potentialities of work, in terms of their prospect for fulfilling these human needs.
3. Identify and communicate these prospects and potentialities to people in terms of their aims, needs, and aspirations.
4. Demonstrate a sensitivity and continuity of interest in people, their motivations, and their progress toward these mutually understood goals.

Understanding Your People

Decades ago — long before studies and understanding of employee motivation and operant behavior had reached their current sophisticated state — personnel men recognized that there was value in interrelating the aims and ambitions of employees with the jobs and prospects which a company had to offer. Therefore, many old application forms contained a question, "What are your professional aims and objectives?"

Because studies had not yet revealed the true significance of this information, it was treated rather off-handedly by both personnel managers and job applicants. Personnel managers regarded the information purely on surface value and tried, insofar as possible, to hire and place people in terms of the similarity or compatibility of job prospects to people's stated objectives. Job candidates, for their part, recognizing this effort on the part of their interviewers, tried hard to reflect carefully phrased objectives which would have selling effect in their similarity to prospects and needs of the work for which they were applying.

The simple question "Why?" can transform this superficial information into fundamental and useful personnel data. "Why?" may, in fact, support the conclusion reflected by the stated individual objective or aspiration. And when it does, it elaborates the meaning and the composition of the objective enough to make it usable, applicable, and dependable. For instance, in answering "Why?" with regard to the stated objective of "being an engineer," one person may indicate actual content of the job, and may elaborate ". . . because I like to work by myself." It is then possible to determine whether or not the job, environment, and its future prospects fit to this individual's aspirations and expectations. It also becomes clear that, for the moment at least, this employee is not seeking group interaction, supervisory or managerial responsibility, or promotion out of engineering into broader and less specific responsibility in general management. Or another engineer candidate may answer, "... to make a social contribution" — which suggests that engineering may be regarded as a stepping stone, and that he will ultimately move readily into assignments which he regards as having potential for increasing or clarifying his social contribution.

A doctor is a doctor — but "why?" Several of the more obvious objectives which lead a man or woman to select medicine as a career are:

  a) scientific or biological interest;
  b) concern for people — or social service;
  c) "hero worship" — having had a doctor as an idol or ideal;
  d) expected community position, social status, prestige, or income.

Despite the fact that the basic motivations differ, each may lead to comparably successful results and practice, but with differing developments and emphasis. The significant point is that the objective of "being a doctor" is founded on very different compulsions, and these compulsions in turn are all very clear in the interest and personality patterns of the individual employee. Compulsions and objectives are, in reality, interpretation given by the individual to the directions of his interest and personality needs and how he believes these may be most suitably fulfilled.

Aims and Objectives Must Be Realistic

In addition to knowing clearly what these compulsions and objectives consist of, the supervisor must carefully consider:

  a) Are these compulsions related to an accurate assessment of the realities of the work and its prospects?
  b) Are the objectives suitable to the capabilities and potentialities of the individual?

It is vitally important that the supervisor assure this accuracy on both counts. It is the extent to which these basic interests, interest compulsions, and personality needs are found and fulfilled within the occupation — and *not* the occupation itself — which gives to people both sustained continuity in work motivation *and* a sense of self-value and accomplishment in the work and its results. So if the worker's initial beliefs and selection have been erroneous, demotivation will inevitably result.

What we therefore must know about people, in order to understand them adequately goes deeper than the superficial manifestation of their choice of job, work, or profession.

a) What is the underlying reason, interest, personality need of the individual on which he has based his decision and selection of work and profession?

b) Is the occupational choice appropriate: can it currently or potentially fit and fulfill the interest and personality needs of the individual?

c) Does the current — or anticipated — assignment of the employee fit suitably to his interest compulsions?

d) Are the occupational objectives of the individual based on knowledge of the realities of the work, or on a fictional or romantic image of what it may contain, do, or contribute?

e) Are work objectives based on a realistic estimate of the mental, physical, and emotional capabilities and potentialities of the employee?

The five "common instruments" by which the necessary facts and information can be obtained are:

1. interview,
2. study,
3. psychological testing,
4. follow-up, and
5. observation.

The best and most meaningful results are attained when all five instruments are used. And the results fully justify the time, effort, and care which this individual concern necessitates, because along with the understanding which can thereby be obtained, are the indications of motivation, short and long term productiveness, employee needs, as well as the specifics of how the employee will fit in, will do his job, and will develop.

Important Points in Interviewing

Some supervisors and managers regard interviewing as their single most important professional skill. One suggested, "Too many people think about interviewing as something you do only when meeting and screening job candidates. If that were all there was to it, it wouldn't be nearly so important. The fact is that interviewing is something a supervisor does most of every day, not just with job applicants, but with his people, and with others with whom he works. When a supervisor develops a real skill in interviewing, he not only is able to find out all that he needs to know, but he also becomes skillful in putting his ideas across to others."

A common misconception about interviewing is that it is purely a verbal process. Categorically, a trained interviewer is able to make extensive use of nonverbal communication in his interviewing and a major part of the understanding which he derives from interviewing probably pertains to facts which never reached the point of being verbalized.

Interviewing is a direct and voluntary confrontation. Because this is true, both the interviewer and the interviewee approach this experience with an intensified awareness and sensitivity. This is why one of the essentials in successfully conducting interviews is to put the interviewee as much at ease as possible.

In effect, the interviewer is trying to assess the qualifications, responsiveness, and harmony with which the individual will fit into the environment and requirements of the department, occupation, program, or project. And the interviewee is trying to assess what the physical and human environments are, and how comfortably and responsively they will fit to him.

Sensitive Consideration Is Vital

During a session of an extension course on "Human Behavior and Supervision" conducted for the University of New Hampshire, one supervisor-student asked, "What about shock tactics in interviewing? To be fully effective an interviewer must arouse responsiveness on the part of the interviewee. Frankly, as hard as I've tried, I haven't had much success in getting response from the people whom I interview. So in looking around, I've read of a 'shock technique' in which you call the interviewee a liar, or something else which will antagonize and arouse him. Is this a good way to interview?"

The class, consisting entirely of supervisors and managers with five to 25 years of practical and applied experience, debated the technique for the better part of an hour. Their conclusion, cited by the senior member of the group, was: "This may work with a limited number of verbal, poised, and outgoing people, and people who occupationally seek confrontation and challenge. And it might be especially appropriate where the working demands and environmental needs are for aggressiveness, self-assertiveness, and a tough hide. But for the average guy and the average situation, it is potentially disastrous."

A Two-Way Street

Good interviewing is two-way communication. You are seeking both with words and with close observation to understand the interviewee. At the same time, you are trying with words, gestures, inflection, and attitudes to communicate to the interviewee. What he interprets from this personal confrontation becomes the interviewee's enduring assessment of you, what kind of a guy and what kind of boss you are. Using such a shock device will inevitably make him feel that you are a hostile and insensitive guy; it will take years of patient and continuous effort to get this impression out of his mind — if, in fact, you are able to accomplish it at all.

This class then developed a set of simple guidelines for interviewing, which other supervisors in a number of companies and industries have found helpful:

1. Take the initiative in interviewing, using both verbal and non-verbal forms of communication.
   a) Try to utilize an office or an area which is reasonably private and non-distracting — a place familiar to the interviewee, if he already is one of your employees.
   b) Avoid all trickery or appearance of trickery, such as lights, chair placement, discomfort, unusual chair-heights, electronic gadgetry, visual or voice recording.
   c) Extend a friendly and extensive manner, but not one which is unnaturally effusive, or is out of character for you.
   d) Commence the interview with generalities, or comments which do not require answers or a high degree of retentiveness.
   e) Select favorable factors in the individual's background, application, or work record, to denote a sensitivity and interest in the positive aspects which the interviewee has to offer.
2. Use a sampling technique in asking questions.
   a) Select, first, questions or areas in which the individual can usefully contribute information without becoming too involved, exposed, revealed.
   b) Note the kinds of questions to which the interviewee responds most comfortably, fluently, and interestedly.
   c) Return to such "comfort questions" whenever other avenues of discussion appear to produce tension, anxiety, or reluctance.

3. Allow adequate time for the interview, and for the interviewee to relate things of special interest or pertinence to him.
4. Bridge verbal gaps.
    a) Sensitively, and without apparent opinion or bias, test several conclusions with various words in exploring needs about which the interviewee finds difficulty verbalizing.
    b) Use indirectness in dealing with non-verbality, when areas seem particularly sensitive; for instance, cite anonymous cases which you have personally encountered, and which have had favorable conclusions.
5. Terminate the interview on a positive note, which in some way identifies the person and the interview in a favorable light.

The Worker's Self-Image — Key to His Motivation

The worker's self-image differs considerably from his aims and objectives, and provides a much more accurate forecast of how he will react to differing situations, and how he can be motivated, as well as the ultimate direction his responses will take. Self-image is how a man sees himself; objectives are goals which he has selected and toward which he aspires. Actually, objectives may be a good starting point for discovering and delineating a person's self-image. Repeated and paraphrased questions of "why," asked in relation to the objectives — what they mean, and why they were selected — ultimately can reveal the values, the concepts, and the reasons upon which the objectives have been based. In this, the self-image commences to emerge and clarify.

Put in the simplest and bluntest terms, when you know a man's self-image, you understand the man. But until you know it, you do not adequately know the man. This is worth the sensitivity, thought, and patience it takes to discover this aspect of the individual employee. Your goal toward motivating a worker can be fully achieved:

1. If you know the self-image of the individual;
2. If you find that self-image to be healthy and realistic in terms of the man's capacities and potentialities; and
3. If you are able to identify that self-image and its fulfillment in the work, situation, or potentiality which you offer and represent.

This is not to suggest that self-image is easy to discover and explore. Actually, most often an individual's self-image is not rigidly fixed, clear, or coherent; instead, it is made up of a number of very specific and unchanging parts that do not necessarily fit together in a comprehensible total picture. It much resembles a child's kaleidoscope which has a number of rigid and unchanging particles which combine for different pictures as circumstances are changed — as the kaleidoscope is rotated.

A supervisor who devotes the necessary time and patience to discover and understand a worker's self-image not only attains the capacity to motivate the employee, but valuably assists the employee, as well. Until the various fixed particles of a man's self-image form into a logical, rational, and attainable pattern and acquire a degree of constancy and consistency, that worker cannot attain his self-image and thus cannot meet the demands it places on him.

As the supervisor explores the details of the employee's self-image, identifying each fragment with some aspect of the work, the pattern of self-image begins to take clearer and more constant form. In effect, the supervisor guides the employee into channels in which he can find fulfillment and fruition of a wide variety of his individual self-needs. A supervisor-manager thereby motivates the employee, gives him a direction for the full focus and force of his varied needs, and enables a worker's appropriate goals to be clear enough to reflect the means and development by which they can be attained. For example, when a suitable current or prospective occupation is selected to fulfill the self-image needs of the employee, it immediately becomes apparent what he must do to prepare for it, or to gain the necessary skills or educational background which that occupation will require.

— A Compelling Force and Need

Whether or not we recognize it, all of us are impelled by the demands and needs of self-image. Until we understand this, recognize what it consists of, we are necessarily driven by a compulsion which we can neither understand nor clearly fulfill. Attainment of one aspect or fragment of self-image does not give a sense of satisfaction, but shifts our sense of need to another aspect or fragment which has not been concurrently fulfilled. Discontentment, lack of satisfaction, and erratic interest and behavior are bound to result. But when the total pattern of self-image is understood and correlated, attainment in each aspect gives us a sense of progress toward total fulfillment.

Rational or not, clarified or not, attainable or not, self-image inevitably governs a major part of the compulsions, attitudes, and goals in work. As was true in the case of Eddie Boulanger, misunderstood self-images and misdirected self-image compulsions can be disturbing and costly to a company, as well as disastrously destructive to the potentialities of highly capable employees.

Eddie was quite a headache to the small company in which he worked. He had high potentiality, and a total unwillingness to undertake the training or dedication which would enable him to develop and attain this potential. Eddie had been with this employer for six years. At first he had done excellent work, but in the succeeding time, his performance had degenerated; his work was poor, his attitude was worse, he was reporting 72 hours of work a week, and accomplishing what might have been expected in 30 hours or less.

When I met privately with Eddie to discuss the problem, and reminded him of the high potential his current and prior employers believed him to have, he replied, "Look, if I've got potential, let them pay me for it *now*. In the first place, I haven't got time for all that training and development stuff. In the second place, my problems are *right now* — not in some vague future period in which I *might* be paid more if I gave up all my personal time and busted my butt taking all kinds of stupid courses and training. I need it right now!

"Want to know about it? . . . I'll tell you. When I first came to work for this joint I had no problems; I lived in the lower rental area. I was cock-of-the-walk; I made more dough than anybody else on the block. Then, problems: we joined the country club — there's a thousand bucks a year. Having joined it, a new problem, because you can't mingle with all those nice people and live in the place we did. So we bought a house in a good area — there's 45 thousand bucks; and in that nice area and with all those nice people at the club you can't appear in the jalopy I was driving — so I bought a Cadillac. *Somebody* has got to pay for it all." Eddie was trying to live up to a distorted self-image without earning it.

As it was helpless to talk further about potential and lack of dedication, I asked, "But Eddie — how about the 72-hour-a-week bit? You know darn well that there isn't that much to do — and you aren't turning out that much work!" Eddie grinned, "Oh, that's simple. Look, I figured out what it costs me to live per year. I divide that amount by my hourly rate, and it shows me how much time I've got to put in. And I'll tell you something — this 72 hours isn't enough any more; my costs are going up. I've got to go to 78 hours!"

Whether or not an employer reaps the benefits of motivation which can be turned on through sensitive understanding and identification of these human needs, the company inevitably pays in one way or another for the worker's self-image. As an interesting positive case, I recently tried to explore the self-image and aspirations of a worker who bluntly replied, "Gee, I don't know. This company and my boss have so far exceeded all my personal ambitions and expectations that I just sort of leave it up to them. They know my capacities and potentialities — and those of the company — better than I do. And they do a wonderful job of guiding me and making it all fit together."

Exploring a Worker's Aims, Hopes, and Expectations

There are actually three guiding forces which influence an employee's general attitudes and reactions in and toward work: the first is how he visualizes himself — his self image; the second is how he visualizes his work — or his expectations; the third is how he visualizes his self-image and expectations identified in the work — his "motivation".

How the individual visualizes his work, what his expectations are in relation to work depend heavily on the early education and guidance he has had relating to his work concepts. People are heavily influenced by their parents in what their work attitudes and expectations are and become. And this is especially true when parents have been engaged in similar work, or if the parents are strongly identified in the selection and education of the occupation of the worker. Similarly, there is strong influence on interest, occupational choice, and concept of work instilled in people at very early and all subsequent years in their education, as well as in and by community attitudes to which they are exposed. In a single-industry town, for instance, strong positive or negative attitudes — and specific visualization and expectancies — are built early in life, particularly among workers whose parents have been directly or indirectly involved with that industry.

This is a fact of life which requires thought and exploration before a supervisor can adequately know his people and know what to expect of them. It also is a highly useful thing to remember in determining the communications and orientation needs of each person who is hired and assigned.

How Testing Can Help — or Hinder

In my own professional activity, I need to understand people quickly and accurately, in order to assess and promote the mutual best interests of the managed and the managers. For this purpose, I have used certain selected psychological tests for many years, with the voluntary participation of company employees. Of the many thousands of people who have cooperated with me in these tests, very few — possibly three or four — have indicated disagreement with the conclusions and interpretations. Virtually all have strongly expressed their agreement with the findings, and their belief in the great personal value and guidance they received through their participation.

My selection of these particular tests — one an interest test, and the other an audit of personality — was based on my own infinite and devout belief in people, and in people potential. More than 30 years of professional observation of people have led me to daily increase my respect for people, and for their infinite potential.

This is a "people belief" which also makes me publicly ridicule the pessimists and detractors who speak derogatorily of ethnic or racial differences, of "cranial sizes," and of "brain weights." The fact is that, to date, less than six percent of the human brain has been developed and used — which suggests to me that the remaining 94 or 95 percent is a sound estimate of our development potentialities. Perhaps three or four thousand years from now — when we have developed and utilized much more of the remaining 94 or 95 percent — it will be feasible to discuss relative "brain weights" and "cranial capacities." But for the moment, it is appropriate only to speak of people potential — and it is negative, inane, and irrelevant to speak only or predominantly of "human limitations."

The Infinite People Potential

Within the wide range of normalcy — and mental and emotional health — people potential is infinite. One of the greatest wonders to me is that never a day passes in which I do not learn more, and become more amazed at how infinite the potential of people truly is. And I have yet to meet a person whose potential is not vastly beyond that which he believes it to be. To the man or woman who is charged with the responsibility for supervising and developing people, and who can see and assess people in this realistic light, the challenge and the assurance are overwhelming, because to be responsible for developing and applying the infinite people potential means that the personal and professional attainments of the sensitive supervisor are truly beyond estimate.

People can do anything — provided their efforts and directions are supported by their interest and their personality structures. So the tests which I utilize were selected to assist in assuring that people's efforts are being directed along lines supported by their interest and personalities. Similar tests are used in many high schools in order to assist in the vocational and occupational guidance which these schools provide to their next-scheduled graduating class.

In theory — thus when other factors of reality need no consideration — occupations should be selected which conform precisely to all the positive interests and personalities of people. But the hard fact is that occupations cannot (yet) be tailored and geared entirely to individuals. Men and women acquire experience in fields and activities which do not necessarily lie within the scope of their positive interests. This latter is a "vested" and "salable" experience and thus must be applied and capitalized, in order to give people full value and return from the time and experience of their prior employment.

In reality, therefore, most men and women will find that not all aspects and requirements of their work and assignments will have the support of their positive interests. Some aspects of work may be in areas in which a person may even have strong disinterest or disinclination. If the predominant content of work does interest a person, he must then accept the negative areas. And in the performance of work, an employee should consciously concentrate on doing proficiently in the negative interest areas: positive interests are strengths and supports, and will largely take care of themselves; negative areas require conscious and conscientious attention.

Helping Workers' Self-Fulfillment

Positive interests are compulsions — and are occupational strengths — but also they are demands on the individual, and on his occupation and social pursuits. To the extent that positive interests apply and are satisfied within or through the occupation, a man or a woman will be a motivated worker, and will find self-value, self-worth, and fulfillment in the assignment. But when strong positive interests are not encompassed and fulfilled by an occupation, these represent unsatisfied demands. To achieve balance, the man or woman should specifically seek active fulfillment of these unsated interests through outside work, hobbies, recreation, or social activities.

When all positive interests are fulfilled by the occupation, or when a life-style is developed in which personal and non-occupational activities are planned to supplement and complete the active utilization of positive interest, the individual finds a sense of well-being. Unless strong positive interests are actively fulfilled in either occupational or personal spheres, or in the combination of the two, an unrest ultimately develops which diminishes the person's effectiveness and sense of personal fulfillment.

Psychological tests can sometimes be of immense help. But testing also can hinder — or even have disastrous effects — if it is not used wisely, sensitively, and competently. Commenting on tests administered to him shortly after he was employed by a company in the Cleveland area, a young draftsman said, "I was never told the results — what they indicated. So they made me nervous. I was sure that something had gone wrong, that otherwise they would have told me about them. I really felt like a sitting duck; no matter what I did, there were those tests waiting in the personnel files to come out and haunt me.

"I worked for that company for five years. But with my concern about the tests, I imagined all sorts of things, such as that I was being held back and bypassed. Finally I could take it no longer, and I quit. A year or so later, I called that company's personnel office, explained that I no longer worked for the company, never would, and that I would like to know the test scores. I found that they were extremely favorable. If I'd known that, I never would have left the company."

There is a certain mystique about psychological tests. People feel that they are somewhat naked and exposed until they know and have been reassured about the result, and how the finding will be used. The best overall results are attained:

1. When people know in advance the underlying purpose and reason for the tests;
2. When they know how the test scores will be used, and by whom;
3. When tests are undertaken voluntarily and on a cooperative and mutual interest basis;
4. When test scores and interpretations are fully reported and discussed with the cooperating employee; and
5. When all facts pertaining to the test and testing are handled with sensitive appreciation for the thoughts and feelings of the employee.

In my own experience I have found that test scores are actually of greater value to the employee than to the company. After all, the worker has a greater vested interest in the test and what it reveals than does the company. To him, they reflect a large measure of his total ability, suitability, and future; to the company, it is one of a set of test scores and what they indicate are a pretty minor consideration, when calculated in terms of the percentage which one man represents in the total company work force. Tests handled with sensitive candor can be immensely helpful in guiding a man in the proper direction, helping him to avoid missteps, and indicating to him how he can best supplement and strengthen the job-requirement areas in which he is weak or inadequate.

As Foresight in Forestalling Problems

Even negative findings can be useful to the participating employee, as well as to the company, if they are viewed and used constructively. Once in privately reviewing tests with cooperating employee Ralph Anderson — tests which indicated that Ralph was extremely well-suited to his occupation in all aspects except one — I said, "Ralph, there is just one thing that you've got to watch out for. The tests suggest that you are extremely emotional, quick-tempered, volatile." Like a bomb-blast, Ralph was out of his chair, screaming, *"I am not!"* Tears were gushing from his eyes as he bolted through the door, slamming it so hard that he broke the glass.

The incident happened almost 20 years ago, and in the meantime, Ralph and I have become good friends. Four times during this period of years, Ralph has retaken the same tests and always with the same results. When considering occupational or employment changes — or even some personal problem — Ralph has usually asked, "In terms of what you see in the tests, do you think I should get involved in this?" And many times he has said, ". . . those darn tests! I don't like what I see — but seeing it, and knowing it, has saved me many, many headaches and heartaches!"

Sensitivity in handling both the administration and reporting of tests is highly essential, for tests get very close to the well-guarded domain of people's inner thoughts and feelings. Favorable results in psychological testing demand that they be administered with sensitivity and understanding for the feelings and reactions of the participant; that the purpose, meaning, and ultimate use of these tests be clearly explained. It also necessitates a report, analysis, and interpretation of test scores and meanings. Otherwise the value may be lost, or the testing may have adverse effects which could more than outweigh the value of their findings.

Experience As a "Vested Interest"

At 54 years of age, and as partner and part-owner in an internationally operated engineering firm, George Graham felt discontented and dissatisfied, or, as he described it, he had "a bad case of malaise." George was second generation management rather than a founder; he had entered the firm with five years' experience, after attaining his B.S. in engineering with summa cum laude class standing, and had subsequently achieved his M.S. in engineering.

Tests of George's interests and personality showed that he had followed an ill-chosen career pattern from the outset. His interests in mechanical, scientific, and computational activity were markedly negative. His scorings in persuasive, people, and supporting personality patterns reflected an interest in interpersonal relations and selling. George had literally lived by determination and resolve, rather than interest, and a shift to customer service, contact, and selling removed his sense of uneasiness and malaise. To fully utilize his engineering know-how and the "vested interest" of long experience, he served as a prime sales representative for the engineering firm of which he was a partner.

Lindley Bowen was hired by a consumer goods company primarily as a sympathetic move, when he was released by a concern for which he had worked almost 30 years in an allied industry, and was tentatively assigned to the sales department. Lindley's tests suggested that he had a wide range of interests, most of which were in relatively low degree — but about the only field in which he could *not* work happily and productively was sales. Basically he was more geared to accounting, finance, and administration. Hearing of the test conclusions, Lindley bristled, "But I have been in sales for over 25 years. As a matter of fact, for the last 15 I've been a sales V.P."

Investigation showed that the reason Lindley had been released was that the company's sales record had been so poor that the concern was precariously near bankruptcy. And it was also discovered that Lindley had a nervous tic and, had been under treatment for several years for an ulcer. Reassigned into administration, where his administrative and computational interests were utilized and his sales experience was applied in report and analysis of sales and marketing, his health and well-being rapidly improved.

He later commented, "Sure, I go along with the tests, their validity and their accuracy, and the fact that a man's potential can only be fully realized in the area of his positive interest. But I'd like to inject three new job-words into your vocabulary: *caprice, opportunism,* and *politics.* I started off in accounting and administration where the tests correctly reflected I should be. A job opened up for which the marketing director chose me — that was *caprice.* When the sales manager resigned without notice, I was on the inside track — that was *opportunism.* To assure that I got the job, I approached the president and the executive vice president at their homes that night — that was *politics.*"

His occupational assignment, experience, and progress were not unique. Others have similarly digressed from the path of their interests for similar opportunities. Business circumstances, economic opportunities, and the demands in a man's life strongly influence his occupational pattern, and often build a "vested interest" of experience which he feels he cannot abandon without going back and starting all over. As Mr. Bowen concluded, "When there is no occupational guidance and planning, momentary circumstances soon entice you so far out on a limb that there is no turning back — yet, logically, such a course is almost inevitably foredoomed to failure and to really basic problems."

Observing and Understanding Workers' Responses

Tests are extremely valuable, both to the supervisor-manager in understanding his people, and to his people in understanding themselves. They help to clarify and validate workers' needs, and thus to assist the supervisor-manager in selecting the appropriate assignment and environment of work, and in orienting workers to the reason for the selection and the ways in which it will identify with and fulfill their motivational needs. But tests still are merely an instrument which is useful when a supervisor-manager is constructively endeavoring to understand his people. Equally, and as an essential supplement to testing, observation of employee responses, as well as basic individual study and interview of works, is a high-yield and essential aspect of supervisory administration.

As in testing, a large measure of the success of observation depends on the open-minded constructiveness, positivism, and objectivity with which it is undertaken. Approached in this manner, the process and findings both are of mutual interest to the supervisor and to the worker, and thus can enlist the vitally important participation and favorable response of the employee. Conversely, the very first sign of negativism inspires negativism in the attitude of the worker, and converts participation into belligerent refusal to co-operate. Perhaps equally as important, preconceived ideas have a tendency to prove themselves, no matter how erroneous they may be, because they close one's mind to alternatives, as well as to reasons, rationale, and explanations.

7

HELPING AND STIMULATING
YOUR GROUP TO WORK TOGETHER

Going over the list of registrants for an extension course on "The Fundamentals of Supervision," I was surprised to find the name of a Ph.D. candidate. Educational levels of other enrollees varied, but this young man's academic background far exceeded that of all the other students. When I inquired about his interest in the course, the young engineer explained, "I've heard that all the men and women enrolled are experienced and practicing supervisors and I felt that I might be able to learn from them what supervision actually is all about, what it consists of, and whether or not I should plan to train for supervisory assignment."

Reminded that he was listed as manager of a good-sized plant, he explained that it was a research facility; thus, despite its size and capital investment, it was operated by only four men — himself and three others. Although he was designated as the chief of the operation, he and his companions all were working independently on different projects; assignments were clearly described and the four men reported individually to four different project managers. They "cooperated" — but he had no responsibility for guidance, scheduling, or teamwork.

After the ten weeks of the course, discussions with classmates, and the assistance of a series of psychological tests, the young engineer felt that he had adequately sized up himself and the responsibilities of supervision. His conclusion was that he was best-suited for a profession in research — one in which he would either work by himself, or collaborate with others, but in which he would not have responsibility for supervising other people.

"I have great respect for these folks who are suited for supervision," he said, "They are patient, sensitive, and understanding. I'm more subject-oriented, and a supervisor must be people-oriented. However, I don't think that we should minimize the role and the importance of the 'lone-worker,' either; each has a vitally necessary contribution to make. We seem inclined invariably to try to multiply talents. If a man has a skill which is important, we feel that we should magnify his values and results by requiring him to teach, guide, and supervise others in these same skills. But some people do not have the interest or personality to enable them to effectively transmit their skills through others — and some kinds of skills must be applied directly and individually by the men who possess them. I'm a 'lone worker' — but I think you'll find many people in my profession who are like me."

When Talented People Don't Fit

Merrill Young is also an engineer. Clever, effective, innovative, and accurate as an engineer, he does an appallingly poor job in supervision. Merrill antagonizes people. He has been temporarily and tentatively assigned a number of times as a supervisor in a wide variety of situations. And in each group to which he was assigned, decreased productivity, low morale, quits, transfer requests, and "no shows" have immediately resulted.

In his own words, Merrill assessed the situation: "I have neither the time nor the patience for people who are not willing or qualified to work. If I tell a man once to do something, he should do it; if he doesn't and quits, that saves me the trouble of firing him. And if I tell him once to do something, he should either be able to do it, or he should get fired — because it shows that he either can't or won't understand."

To be completely fair in evaluating Merrill's capacities and performance, we must recognize that the very facts and personality traits which make Merrill an excellent individual or "lone worker" are the same ones which make him a chronic failure as a supervisor, or in any other occupation in which his prime responsibility is that of working *with* or *through* people. Merrill's attitude toward himself is exactly the same as that which he reflects toward other people: he is impatient, exacting, driving, inconsiderate, ruthless. Applied to himself, this means excellence, perfection, and precision in his work and results. Applied to other people, it means every negative human response short of mayhem and of homicide.

Putting Occupational and Talent Values in Proper Perspective

Why then — with such obvious individual talents and contributions as Merrill and the extension course student had to make — should such people seek responsibilities for supervision? Part of the reason for this is the extent to which management has single-mindedly valued vertical promotion and supervisory-management position, made them the sole criterion of success and progress. This emphasis implies that vertical promotion and supervisory position are the only hallmarks of progress and accomplishment; it minimizes the progress which an individual may make in occupational skills, craftsmanship, broader activity within the same talent areas.

The impact of the vertical promotion valuation on the individual worker is tripled by the sources of influence which he finds coercing him. First, it is the company itself: within the company there is often an attitude of disdain toward employees who fail to seek and attain "promotion into supervisory responsibility"; in some companies there are relatively serious consequences for the employee who fails to earn or accept the challenge and promotion. Secondly, by being identified with industry, success and progress for the worker are necessarily judged by his community in the promotional terms and measurements that industry publishes as its success criteria, and so the individual finds himself pressured outside the company to earn the success hallmarks of the company. Finally, the worker is coerced by his own feelings and responses. Every human being seeks some sense of self-worth and progress. When no alternative marks of attainment are offered, a man must work toward the arbitrary symbols no matter how undesirable or unsuitable they may be *to* him or *for* him.

This is not to suggest that we depreciate the increasing value, need, and impact of talented supervision. To the contrary, it is meant to emphasize both the value of supervision and the crucial need to limit supervisory assignment to those men and women who have the talent, interest, and capability to act as leaders. Supervision must be a matter of careful selection, not just an award for technical competence or long service. It is important to the proper selection of supervisory people, as well as to the support which supervisors secure from master technicians, that the contribution of both natures of occupation be valued and respected.

We must recognize the contribution made by non-supervisory workers, craftsmen, professionals, at all levels. All skills and occupations must be recognized and valued for their own specific contribution. Occupational values must receive adequate recognition so that the incumbent's effort, and accomplishment can be rewarded with a valid sense of self-worth, contribution, and progress. Without this, there is necessarily a compulsion to seek the goal of supervisory assignment, and there is not enough support of the value of non-supervisory occupation to provide motivation and stimulation to high-standard performance.

Occupational Values Have Changed

Actually, the single-minded belief that everyone should aspire to supervisory position is a throwback to old-time management concept before supervision attained professional level, and before non-supervisory jobs had become as technical and complex. Failure to recognize these fundamental changes can lead to serious consequences.

"I can't go along with this modern management theory," a hard-nosed mid-west plant superintendent argued. "Anyone can be a good supervisor — and should want to be one. The best way to develop a good supervisor is to pick a good worker — one who has set a good example, one who is really interested in his work. Pick him out, 'throw him to the wolves' — within a month you'll know whether he's got guts and steam enough to make the grade."

In the plant operating under the jurisdiction of this superintendent, annual turnover at the time was running in excess of 70 percent, turnover among supervisors was at an equivalent rate, and no foreman, supervisor, or lead man had been in management assignment longer than 19 months.

Discovering and Understanding the Lone Worker

Such trial by fire approach in differentiating the lone worker, team worker, team leader, and the man or woman with supervisory talent is unjustified, hazardous, and unwise. It is unjustified because there are a number of techniques and methods by which each group can be distinguished with reasonable accuracy, and usually people themselves are clear in their own minds as to how they prefer to work — if their natural inclinations are not distorted by the single-minded goals we have just discussed. (And, of course, we sometimes become so intensely concerned about key vacancies that we become inclined to "over sell" the idea of promotion, against our own better judgment and that of the employee.) "Trial by fire" is precarious because of the disruption it can cause in the established and harmonious coordination of a work group, and because of the permanent damage it can do to the worker's attitude, sense of well-being, and relationship with others in the work group. And it is unwise because the conclusions reached through such experimentation are not necessarily valid.

The man who is on trial is necessarily tense, and his tension is passed along to the work group, as well as distorting his own performance and accomplishment. Rarely can brief experiments be fair and conclusive because the men or women being "tried" usually are in a controlled situation — and thus are seldom given the latitude to truly and fully apply their ideas and efforts.

"To make such an experiment work, for it to be fair and valid, you've got to give a person free rein," a construction superintendent suggested. "You must give him freedom and latitude to make mistakes. Actually, it's in the area of mistakes that you find your most valid answers. First, for example, does a man exercise judgment in trying to find out what he does know? Does he ask questions? And second, when he does make mistakes, does he learn from them? In my opinion such experimentation should be used only after you have become reasonably certain that a new employee *wants* to be a supervisor and has the basic knowledge it will require, and have found that he and people interact favorably with each other."

Given time for adequate observation, the experienced supervisor generally is able to discern from an individual's interaction with other employees his pattern of job-choice, and his mode of working, and whether the employee is most suitably:

a. an individual or "lone" worker,
b. a group worker and team-member, or
c. a suitable candidate for future supervisory assignment.

And it is vitally important to know the answers to these questions — not only for the purpose of appropriately distributing the work load, but for securing productive departmental interaction, motivating individual employees, and accurately planning and projecting the structure and future capability of the department.

Miscasting employees into ill-fitting roles or job situations causes several rather distinct problems. In one recent study of a company organization, I found that several key problems in finished goods classification and inventory, in invoicing, in shipping and delivery dates, and in report and evaluation of returned goods, all centered in the relationship between the warehousing-shipping department and the office, sales, production, and packing functions. Examining the problem more closely as it related to these latter functions, I discovered that the degree of difficulty appeared in direct ratio to the length of service of the particular supervisor. It was less of a problem to senior supervisors, and was extremely frustrating to relatively new appointees.

Then, revealing comments commenced to crop up about Henri LaBonte, who for the past 16 years had been shipping-warehousing supervisor. Universally supervisors said, "Henri's a real nice guy," and "Henri knows every nut, screw, bolt, and product in the place." But additional remarks suggested: "He keeps it all to himself"; "He never writes anything down"; "You never can get any answers from Henri"; "He never pays any attention to suggestions"; "You never can get any suggestions from him"; "Henri doesn't say much — or tell you anything"; "He works like a Trojan — but he never seems to relate himself or his work to anyone else or anything else."

Reporting to Henri on the scores of three psychological tests he had taken, I told him that the tests suggested that he was in entirely the wrong job: that he appeared to have strongly negative interest-response toward clerical, computational, record-keeping, interaction responsibilities; that he seemed to prefer being a "lone worker." I explained that his interests, preferences, and personality patterns seemed ideally suited to independent work in a machine shop.

Henri's face was beaming as he said, "Look — will you please write all of this up — and give it to me in three copies? I want one copy for my wife and one for my boss. I've been telling them all this for years — and maybe this will make them see and understand. I wish I'd had a chance to take these darn things 20 years ago!"

Helpful Aids in Formulating Accurate Conclusions

Selected psychological tests can help in discovering which of these three patterns best suit an employee's interests and preferences. For instance, the combination of the Kuder Preference Vocational and Kuder Preference Personal tests — particularly when used in conjunction with sensitive tests of personality traits and patterns — provides some sound basic indications from which to formulate suitable and accurate conclusions.

But whether tests, observations, or work records are used in formulating tentative conclusions, the supervisor should bear in mind that they should be presented to the employee as being merely tentative indications, rather than rigid and fixed conclusions. If an employee is expected to accept and abide by a decision pertaining to him, he should feel that at least in some degree he has participated in the formulation of that decision. This is equally true whether the decision is that the employee is to stay in his current niche, or that he is to be transferred, trained, or promoted.

My own 35 years of experience with selection and assignment of people — matching people with jobs, occupational situations, and work-groups — may have provided enough variety of people and situations to help me make appropriate and workable suggestions; but it has also made me keenly aware of the possibility of not knowing some particularly vital fact which would influence such decisions.

Furthermore, dogma invites dogma: the supervisor who approaches any aspect of his employee relationships with fixed or pre-conceived ideas — who does not invite and encourage worker-response and participation — is asking for trouble. At best, he will create resentment and a chasm between himself and his subordinates; at worst, he will find that the worker will in one way or another challenge his decision.

There are several human characteristics on which a supervisor can ordinarily rely, which are safeguards of the ultimate accuracy and workability of the decision in which the worker participates. Most important of these is that people do not like to fail, and thus will not insist on being placed in the position in which there is no reasonable assurance of success. Second, people do not like to be embarrassed, which they would be by failure. Third, people like to feel amplified and fulfilled, and will respond favorably to prospects which offer this kind of suitability. Thus, if a supervisor has a record for fairness and sensitivity, and approaches his occupational and classifications problems with an obvious thoughfulness and preparation but an open-minded flexibility, he will usually get from his people the facts, responsiveness, and participation he needs to formulate an accurate conclusion.

Such tests as those mentioned earlier reveal, for instance, the extent to which an employee seeks sociability or is withdrawn, prefers working with people or more singly on projects or idea development. They also suggest the degree to which the individuals are people-oriented and people-sensitive, or, conversely, are inclined to regard people primarily on a use-and-results basis. And they often show whether the degree of interest in the subject area may be significantly stronger than interest in working *with* or *through* people.

Determining What the Worker Really Likes

Leonard Scarborough was applying for a job as a shipping supervisor. Psychological test patterns suggested that Leonard was so intensely interested in clerical activities that he might prefer direct responsibilities in procedures and records activities, rather than instructing and supervising others — and thereby becoming somewhat removed from actual personal involvement in clerical matters. An apparent desire to escape the responsibility for decision-making or decisive interaction with people stimulated several interview questions about the specific aspects of his prior supervisory work; for instance, he was asked what aspects he most enjoyed, and in which parts he had encountered the greatest difficulty.

Leonard answered that he had enjoyed the work itself, that he liked clerical matters, but that he regarded as "a real pain in the neck" the need to try to get things done through other people — or even to get them to cooperate with him in things on which he was working by himself. He felt that "people just don't want to work anymore."

"Being a supervisor of a group just means that you've got all these problems," he continued. "You get work load added and added because you're a supervisor until it gets to the point where you can't do it all yourself. When there's too much to do yourself, and you can't get other people to do it for you or even to help out, the job just isn't fun anymore. If I could just get someone else to do the crew-work and leave me alone, I could do a real good job by myself in getting together all the necessary facts and figures, and in keeping them up to date."

Similarly, Lieutenant Thomas, an Air-Force engineer, complained, "The time-consuming nonsense of trying to get other people to understand and do things! Sure, I'm a supervisor but all that means is that I've got to stand around and hear why Joe can't do a project because he's worried about his teen-age kid or something. I'm a good engineer — and I'd be a lot happier if they'd just give me a direct project, the stuff I need to work with, and freedom to work it out in my own way and at my own pace — and leave this personnel-coddling jazz out of it!"

Whether or not they are supplemented and supported by psychological tests, direct personal interviews with individual employees considerably reduce the time requirements of personal observation — and tremendously diminish the risk of errors and missteps. But to be valid, accurate, and fair, the interviewing supervisor must first develop an open-mindedness toward human values and the contributions which people make through the application of their talents, and a sincere respect for the varied natures of occupations and assignments. The supervisor who has a fixed set of ideas about occupational values, whose attitude toward human talent relates only to supervisory management assignment, and who minimizes the contribution of the lone worker, is one who will not secure accurate and fair results from interviewing.

Be Realistic About Actual Requirements

Among executives especially — but sometimes in supervisory managers, as well — there is at times a tendency to seek more potentiality in people than the current jobs or future possibilities of the department or company actually justify. In a Boston-based company, for example, terrific problems of turnover, poor morale, and low productivity were encountered simply because management consistently followed a policy of selecting exclusively those job-candidates who they felt had ambition, zeal, and high potential for promotion and managerial assignment. Small, and with an annual growth rate of only five percent, the company could not fulfill the promises implied by this policy; promotion possibilities were inadequate, and vacancies in supervisory-managerial positions were too few. Ultimate recognition that 65 percent of the occupations were largely dead-end and unchanging led to a considerable revision of this policy.

As one supervisory manager in the plant later commented, "This operation is largely dependent on people who are interested and happy in routine, repetitive work. When you understand the operation on this basis, you appreciate these people more and motivate them more. I believe that in reviewing workers' potentials, you should do so in terms of their potential for filling your actual current and future needs and requirements, rather than on their potentiality for progress or promotion."

Be Realistic in Determining Your Departmental Needs

Do you really need promotability? Beyond the dictates of your growth and replacement rates, to what extent can you actually sup-

port supervisory managerial potentiality and aspiration among
your work people?

Sometimes, also, we are inclined to underestimate the situations
in which "lone workers" are ideally suited. Mary Crandall, secretary in a one-girl regional office of a large national company, had
done such an excellent job that she was being considered for a "promotion" into the main office. Because the small facility was used as
a training ground, turnover had been high. Yet with different bosses,
sometimes left unsupervised to proceed on her own initiative, Mary
had done extremely well, kept administrative procedures stabilized,
and maintained the flow of essential reports. However, before he
would allow promotional consideration to progress to the point of
decision, the general supervisor insisted that he talk personally and
privately with Mary.

Tests and the general supervisor's interview both showed that
Mary was strictly a "lone worker." As a matter of fact, once this
was revealed, it became clear that one of the reasons that she had
been unperturbed by personnel changes in the office — had consistently retained her pattern of excellence in job performance when
she was unsupervised — was because she was an independent "lone
worker." Her comment to the general supervisor, in confirming the
"lone worker" classification, was: "Thanks for getting me off the
hook. I like it here and want to stay here. Frankly, I would have quit
if anyone had made an issue about promoting me into the general
office."

Perhaps we are inclined to think of "lone workers" only in terms
of people who prefer to be physically separated from other people
— to work "on a desert island," in effect. This is not true, and it is
vital to recognize this, and yet to remember that "lone workers" will
not interact with others and become responsive team-members. And
"lone workers" themselves may sometimes confuse the issue of their
assignments by apparently incompatible interest or personality
traits.

As an example, Gloria Dixon had done an excellent job as a process clerk, in which work she had done a sizable amount of typing
and stenography, with considerable expertise. Psychological test
patterns reflected that she had an extremely high preference for
working in groups of people, but at the same time was withdrawn,
introverted, was not particularly responsive to people, and would
avoid assignments which would require interaction, teamwork, or
supervisory responsibility. Throughout the entire four years of her
assignment with the company, she had been consistently offered

each suitable promotion which became vacant — and quickly and invariably she had refused, and had asked not to be considered.

Due to the sudden serious illness and resignation of a key secretary, Gloria was asked to substitute in the assignment until a replacement could be found. But after three weeks of unsuccessful recruiting for a new secretary, a temporary replacement was hired for Gloria's regular job, and the following Monday morning Gloria's husband called in to report that she had resigned.

A closer look at Gloria's social patterns at work and at home would have made it clear that this would be the outcome of any move to force her into an occupation in which close interaction with other people would be required. At work she rarely took coffee breaks, avoided company recreational activities, left the office each day to have luncheon by herself. The only guests at her home were close relatives and even this degree of socializing was infrequent. Her husband — considerably more sociable than Gloria — belonged to social clubs and engaged in only those activities which he could attend by himself. Gloria's preference was actually working *in* groups of people, not *with* groups of people. Hers was an effort to "get lost in the crowd" — to be inconspicuous because of the presence of other people.

What Leadership Really Means

There have been so many trite descriptions, comments, and generalizations about what leadership means and consists of that we have become impatient with the word. However, leadership is an absolute essential to the future growth and profitability of companies, and it is the major ingredient and vital responsibility of the job of supervisory management. It is thus a basic necessity in any constructive and meaningful discussion of the practice and effectiveness of supervision. When we accept this fact, and face the question of leadership realistically, we find it is not only more essential than we previously recognized, but it is also fun, rewarding, and challenging.

In an article a number of years ago, General Eisenhower synthesized the whole meaning, with the suggestion that "leadership is in terms of people": this clarifies many things — and sets us on a new and more productive course. For instance, the fact that leadership is in terms of people reflects that we must know the people whom we are assigned to lead. And, in turn, this indicates that the most vital and productive aspect of our job and know-how is in our understanding of people.

This definition of leadership gives us a clearer, surer, and updated concept of managing. Most of us remember the old cliche which was used to define "good management practice" — which was said to be by following the Golden Rule. Several years ago I had occasion to sit in on the contract negotiations between a New England company and the representative of the International Union by which the company was organized. Each time in the course of the morning that negotiations became a little sticky, some member of the management negotiating team would comment, "But we follow the Golden Rule!"

At noon, as I walked out of the building with the business agent of the International Union — who incidentally was chief negotiator for the union — he turned to me and said, "King, so help me if they mention that Golden Rule bit just once more we're going out on strike!" Overhearing him, one of the members of the management team said, "What do you mean, go out on strike? We follow the Golden Rule; that's good management practice!"

Slowly and with obvious exasperation, the union representative turned to him and said, "The Golden Rule says 'Do unto others as you would have others do unto you.' We don't want done unto us what you want done unto you, we want done unto us the way we want done unto us!" And in truth and in practice, management's historic use of the Golden Rule did lead many supervisor-managers to try to estimate the wants, needs, values, aspirations, motivations, and questions of subordinates in terms of what they themselves felt they should be. The Eisenhower definition of leadership more clearly and unquestionably bases leadership and effectiveness in managing on the understanding of people.

Viewed in this manner, leadership becomes the answer to a wide variety of needs and compulsions. For instance, leadership is the reverse of the present-day militant cliche "power to the people" — it is power *from* the people. Leadership is the process of arousing and directionalizing human response. Thus, leadership is the understanding and "turning on" of employee motivation: leadership has aptly been called "motivational management."

Leadership is not only the capacity to inspire, arouse, and direct human response; it is also the capacity to coordinate; thus, in more common phraseology, leadership includes the capability to build activated teamwork. In either leadership or motivation, the extent or degree of human response depends on confidence in the leader — and that confidence requires employees' feeling that they "understand the boss," and that he understands them well enough to guide and motivate them in the direction of their own best interests and fulfillment.

As a supervisor sees leadership in terms of his people, he understands more and more why leadership is an increasingly vital element in industry, and why its practice and effectiveness are largely centered in his own job and his own managerial practices. Recognizing the growing human need for leadership and motivation, and how these are becoming more job-centered, an office-machines manufacturing supervisor commented, "People seem to be turning their personal values, self-expression, self-worth, social and social identity questions more and more toward occupations, work, and work relationships. This puts a heck of a burden on the guy who is responsible for supervising people. But if he can see and understand what leadership and motivation really are, his job becomes a lot clearer and more attractive."

It is true that high on the list of employee motivations are "a sense of belonging," "a sense of accomplishment," "a sense of self-worth," "a sense of identity." And as people increasingly seek these in their work and occupations, the responsibility to provide for their fulfillment is clearly crucial. However, as these reflect both human need and the potentiality for acceptance and response to leadership and motivation, they also indicate the immense rewards of sensitive, effective, and understanding supervision — of the supervisor-manager who develops his people potential.

How to Apply Leadership

However, general discussions of leadership have very little practical value until we can list specifically what it consists of, and what people want and expect of us when they accept us and respond to us in a position of leadership. Note that I have said "in a *position* of leadership" — because, clearly, occupation, assignment, prestige, or position do not *establish* leadership, they merely denote that leadership is a responsibility which must be developed and attained in order to fulfill the position requirements.

To develop a valid list of leadership essentials, I sought the suggestions of practicing supervisor-managers attending an extension course which I was conducting in New Haven for the University of Connecticut. The list of items which they suggested was thereafter cross-checked at seminars in 24 regions of the United States, sessions which were attended by more than five thousand supervisors, managers, and executives, collectively representing a wide variety of industries, enterprises, and institutions.

The list is quite clear, and consists of only 20 items, as follows:

1. personal dignity
2. self-respect and respect for others
3. self-confidence
4. ability to appraise human values
5. understanding of people
6. enthusiasm
7. well-founded and consistent work values
8. sensitivity and insight
9. genuine interest in people: empathy
10. interest in new ideas
11. flexibility and perspective
12. fairness
13. humility
14. courage and support
15. knowledge of what is to be accomplished
16. ability to communicate effectively
17. approachability
18. sound judgment
19. dedication to job and company
20. belief — in self and in others

As brief as this list is, it answers numerous questions regarding our practices in managing. For one thing, you will note how clearly this supports the Eisenhower concept of "leadership in terms of people." It suggests to us that people want and need to be led in terms of their individual identities, desires, and aspirations. This in itself answers the often-raised question as to the extent to which management should ask personal questions or use psychological testing or other means to understand the personal backgrounds and make-ups of individual employees. Obviously, in order to achieve an appropriate level of understanding, we must do this and must use all valid devices available to us. We must answer the question of the extent to which we explore personal considerations in terms of the response and reaction of people themselves.

As this list implies, people want and expect to be known by the person who serves as their leader. The really touchy point at issue is that people are concerned as to whether personal information will be used positively and beneficially, or negatively and detrimentally. They must develop a sense of trust that personal information will be used constructively, understandingly, and to their benefit — not to their detriment; thus, they need to know and trust the supervisor before he can, in turn, undertake and exercise this aspect of leadership.

To the experienced supervisor, there is rarely the question or problem of finding out anything he needs to know in order to understand his subordinate personnel. More often, as supervisors have many times told me, the problem is in shutting off the flow of information when it reaches the point of actual need for understanding.

The supervisor-manager who is accessible, sensitive, and keeps his eyes and ears open, finds no major general problem in learning what his people expect from him — or in finding out what he needs to know about them — so long as he has first established a consistent pattern of honesty, sincerity, fairness, and understanding. To achieve this climate of relationship with his workers, a supervisor must:

1. Demonstrate a sincere interest in his people.
2. Indicate his receptiveness and understanding toward people's comments, questions, and meanings.
3. Seek answers to workers' responses, feelings, and information needs.
4. Ask questions tactfully — and in terms of workers' sensitivities and their capacity to understand and communicate.
5. Retain calmness — do not become upset or be judicial or moralizing in response to questions and comments.
6. Frame questions as his own inadequate understanding, instead of inadequacy of clarity of employees' comments and questions.
7. Remain discreet: never comment to one employee about another, either in personal matters, or comments of good or bad performance.
8. Avoid expressing his own opinions and attitudes on matters which are personal to the worker.
9. Answer all questions — or indicate to the employee when he will provide an answer, or that he is unable to do so.
10. Terminate all individual discussions with reassurance of his interest, and of his availability for future discussions.

Your Attitudes — and Values

The crux question, then, is *"What is your attitude toward people?"* Response to your questions and effort to understand people depend on the extent they have seen and learned your positive and constructive attitude and intent, found it consistent enough for them to develop confidence in it and in you.

Two items on the leadership list stimulated an especially high degree of comment and reaction: the first of these is "enthusiasm"; the second is "genuine interest in people: empathy."

At first I became concerned at how frequently and extensively the word "enthusiasm" crept into discussions with non-supervisory people about the general topic of leadership. So one day I asked a long-service bench worker in a paper mill, "Why do you stress enthusiasm so much? And why do you feel that your supervisor should have specific enthusiasm for you and for your job, especially when he has a variety of occupations and people to similarly supervise?"

Her reply was very direct and unhesitant: "To begin with, you must recognize that the value of your job and your attitude toward it is largely that which is reflected by your boss: the supervisor is the one who sets and enforces the standards, and thus he is the one who sets and retains the values which you find in doing it. For a job to be of value to you, it must clearly be of value to your boss; for you to feel a sense of importance in accomplishing your work, you must feel that your boss values the fact that you are assigned to it. You need to have the value of your job and your own effort supported by the attitude reflected by your boss. You need to feel in the reaction of your supervisor that your job has value, and that he values your assignment with it and to it. His enthusiasm is the key to the whole thing."

Another bench worker commented, "It's funny what the boss's enthusiasm does to us. After more than 20 years on the seven-to-three shift, I now find that the shift gets dull and I get tired about one o'clock in the afternoon. About that time, the boss walks through the department with an air of confidence, understanding, appreciation, and enthusiasm. We seem to draw vitality from his response and enthusiasm, because the one o'clock dullness and tiredness disappear — and suddenly it's the three o'clock end of the shift."

Enthusiasm, then, as an extreme manifestation of response and valuation, gives value and meaning to the job and to the person assigned to it. It becomes very apparent that the effect of a supervisor's leadership is in the direction of human response and value, as well as overall acceptance and dedication. Almost invariably the enthusiastic supervisor has an active and animated work crew; the apathetic, disinterested supervisor almost invariably is found to head up a crew whose attitudes and reactions are very similar to his own.

Inspiring and Guiding Responsiveness

Many years ago, before I learned the overwhelming drama of the New York City five o'clock rush hour, I arrived one day at Grand Central Terminal on the train from out-of-state, in answer to a "Help Wanted" advertisement. The address given in the advertisement was in the Times Square area. So, when I saw signs guiding travelers to the crosstown shuttle, I decided to take the subway.

When I arrived on the appropriate subway platform, I was practically alone. It was that mystical hour of five p.m. — so, somehow, before the next train arrived, a crushing mass of people suddenly appeared on the platform. It seemed to me that I lost all sense of self-determination. I couldn't change my mind, move, or select my own direction of motion. When the subway doors had opened, and the last arriving passenger had exited from the train, the phenomenon happened which since then I have always remembered whenever I have heard the phrase "population explosion": without choice or self-determination, the population of that platform "exploded" — and I flowed into the subway car, along with the rest of the surging sea of humanity.

When I was crushed into place, and the doors closed, I found that my left elbow was on a little old lady's head, my left heel was on someone's toe, my right hand was obscuring the face of another passenger, while my upraised right elbow was pushing up the glasses of a tall and extremely muscular looking man. Suddenly I felt extremely ridiculous. I had lost all the "employment motivations" of self-determination, dignity, direction, choice, identity, and seemed even to lose physical dimension in the crush (to be pressed into being thinner and taller). And for what? — merely to save a few minutes walking time. So I started to laugh — and I continued to laugh until the train had almost reached Times Square.

After exiting from the train, I felt guilty. Suppose the ones whom I had most inconvenienced had thought I was laughing at them? So I stopped the two whom I had made most uncomfortable — the elderly lady and the tall gentleman — and said, "I hope you understand that I was laughing at myself, and the situation in which I found myself, and not at any inconvenience I was causing to others!"

The tall gentleman looked at me with a twinkle in his eye, and he said, "No, no one misunderstood. But I learned something from this episode — and I hope that you did, too. I have ridden this car for many years and I've never before seen such a thing happen. Do you realize that your laughing caught on, and that virtually everyone in the train laughed all the way? As a matter of fact, some of them are still laughing!"

The whole point, he suggested, is that in a new situation people feel a *need* to respond and often are uncertain as to what form or direction their response should take. On the one hand, if they saw someone irritated, fighting it, striking out, this would provide an example and guidance of the direction of response; they would follow suit, and there would have been mayhem in the car. But at this moment when they were looking for leadership and direction of response, they heard a laugh, and so this was the direction in which they followed.

He concluded by suggesting, "Somehow there is a 'magic moment' when people are looking for and trying to understand something new, and are seeking an appropriate direction of response — you provided a direction. I think this is something we should all always remember."

As I have told this story in a number of areas, quite a few supervisors have remembered and identified such "magic moments" in their own experience. Sometimes it is in the climax of a series of events which confuse, bewilder, or upset a worker; sometimes it is in relation to a change which has taken place; occasionally it is when something has happened abruptly and unexpectedly; once in a while it happens when a worker feels that he has reached the limit of his capacity to understand. Whatever its cause, these "magic moments for leadership" occur in the lives of all people, represent a peak of susceptibility for leadership and guidance, are symptoms for which experienced supervisors watch, and which they utilize positively, sensitively, and to mutual benefit and best interest.

Long-experienced supervisory managers have found that there are six basic rules essential to recognizing and utilizing these "magic moments" of susceptibility, and successfully and positively applying then the principles of leadership:

1. Bear in mind that the nature and direction of your own response constantly serve as an intensely important communication — and as an example and suggestion of how others within your jurisdiction should act and respond.

2. Keep calm: never lose your temper — or "lose your head."
3. Develop sensitivity for signs of confusion, bewilderment, uncertainty, hesitation, fear, or misgivings among your workers.
4. Devote whatever time is required: do not be impatient or abrupt unless an emergency situation clearly makes it necessary.
5. Gear the time, nature, tone, and content of the discussion sensitively to the worker's needs; be guided by the worker's appearance of understanding and relaxing — and follow up such conferences within two days.
6. Be consistent: remember that a great deal of the response and discipline of your subordinate comes from the self-discipline and sense of purpose they detect in you.

The Importance of Perspective and "Empathy"

Although we have previously touched upon the need to maintain perspective, and for a supervisor to avoid becoming over-personal and involved with his work-people, the need is so vital, and cases in which this error is made are so numerous, that it justifies considerable emphasis and illustration. It is important, too, to recognize that such ill-advised involvement may be occupational or physical, as well as personal or social.

John Sheen had been a member of a pipeline crew for a Texas-based oil company for several years before he was promoted to crew foreman. He told of his own experience in his first day as a supervisor. He was standing on the rim of the trench, watching the crew couple pieces of pipe. Because they were not doing it fast enough or the way he felt they should, he shouted at them — and found, as every supervisor knows, that every time you yell at a subordinate, he "grows another thumb." After ten times of yelling, the crew obviously was "all thumbs." In exasperation, John jumped down in the trench, grabbed the wrench, and did the job himself.

"Before I had completed the work, I heard a voice on the upper rim of the trench, shouting orders to the crew," John commented. "As I looked up I saw the water boy had taken over. This infuriated me so much that I scrambled out of the trench, grabbed the young boy, and was about to shake his teeth down his throat when, suddenly, I realized that he was right and I was wrong. When I jumped down in the trench, I became physically and occupationally involved with my crew. I thus vacated the shoes of the supervisor and became a crew member. All the water boy was doing was merely to step into obviously vacant supervisory shoes."

Maintaining perspective and avoiding excessive personal involvement is a common and vital necessity in all professions which carry responsibility for the response, action, and well-being of people.

After a rather serious automobile accident a number of years ago, I was fortunate to have the services of Dr. Ted Hagerty, a master craftsman in putting accident victims back together again. On one of his visits, I felt that he was being a little bit more relentless than was necessary, and I said, sarcastically, "Ted, do doctors necessarily become calloused and insensitive to the feelings of their patients?"

He pushed back his chair, looked at me intently for several minutes, then said, "King, this is a hard thing for doctors — but it is essential for us to force ourselves to be a little detached, in order to fulfill our responsibilities. Our natural tendency is to understand and feel our patients' feelings and sufferings. When we see and know that pain is intense, it becomes terribly hard to remember that this pain is sometimes an inevitable, essential, and unavoidable part and effect of treatment. It's hard, then, to remember that without this momentary pain *now,* there will be greater and prolonged pain and tragedy *later.*"

Ted went on to explain that to serve as a doctor and a friend, a doctor sometimes must confront a patient with whatever pain as may be unavoidable in order to achieve fullest long-term possible repair and recovery. It's obviously hard to think in long-range terms when pain is so immediate and so evident. But for a doctor to lose his perspective, and become too sympathetically involved in a patient's immediate feelings, is a disservice both as a doctor and a friend.

As a supervisory manager, you must always recognize and remember that your responsibility to people is to see them in perspective so that you can provide them with the perspective they need for their own well-being. Direct personal involvement robs you of your capacity to provide this perspective. In other words, direct personal involvement with your people destroys your capacity to be an effective supervisor.

8

BUILDING JOB VALUES AND
IMPROVING PERFORMANCE

Possibly like many other people, I originally thought of motivation as something workers had only when they were doing something they liked to do, and in an environment in which they enjoyed working. However, this is fortunately a very minor aspect of motivation — and it took a clear-speaking worker and an embarrassing situation to set me straight, to make me understand motivation more broadly and more realistically.

The instance happened a number of years ago while I was working on an assignment for a medium-sized manufacturing concern in Massachusetts. As I was walking through the plant, interviewing groups of workers in each department, one woman, a bench assembler, suddenly said, "You know, you're always yakking about motivation. You ought to talk with Pete Hammond, over there — he's the most motivated worker we have ever seen. Several of the other women at the work bench agreed. And in two or three other parts of the plant I ran into the same comment. So at the end of the plant tour, I sought out the man about whom they were talking.

Introducing myself, I said, "Pete, I understand you are a very motivated worker." To which he replied, "So what?" "So I wanted to talk with you." Bluntly, he said, "So — talk!"

It was at this moment that I made the cardinal error: "What makes you like your job so much?" His face reddened, seemed to swell; there was fire in his eyes as he blurted, "*Like* my job — I *hate* it! Did some nincompoop tell you that I *like* my job? Do you know what my job *is*?" Subdued, I said, "No." Pete then said, "For the last

17 years I have worked for a local janitorial service. My job is to go from plant to plant, cleaning out industrial toilets. *Like* my job — I hate it! And if I ever find anybody who *wants* it, he can have it *right then!*"

Completely shaken, I said, "Pete, I'm sorry!" Gruffly he said, "What are you sorry for?" "Because, Pete, either I have been used as a patsy, or I have unintentionally used you as one." "Why?" "Well, Pete, this motivation bit . . . . " I always felt that his stare was half belligerent and half condescending as he said, "Motivation? Look — are you stupid or something? Don't you know what motivation *means?* Do you think a guy has to *like* his job to be motivated? Sure, I hate my job. It's a lousy, crummy job. But I'm going to tell you something — there's no one in this town who contributes more to the health of industrial employees than I do — not the doctors, not even the public health service!"

Pete's motivation obviously did not center in the *content* of his job, but in the fulfillment of his desire to somehow make a social contribution through his efforts. What I learned from Pete is that motivation may pertain to any one of three major factors of our work:

1. job content,
2. job relationships, and
3. significance of job results.

And what I have since learned is that for a supervisor to "turn on" people and their motivations, he must:

1. Explore and understand the motivations of each individual sensitively and specifically;
2. Identify how these specific motivations can be fulfilled by or in —
   a) job content,
   b) job relationships,
   c) significance of job results;
3. Provide frequent reminders of —
   a) the importance of the job,
   b) the importance of the man and his skills,
   c) the importance of performance, and
   d) the extent to which a man's motivations are being met and fulfilled.

Job Content

If you stop and think about it for a moment or so, you will note the degree to which we emphasize the reward and promotion for the employee doing his work satisfactorily, and ignore job content. This presents no problem when we are dealing with people who are primarily interested in promotion and progress. But what about the people who enjoy the job itself? Are they motivated by and in the assignment?

Four or five years ago, I had the opportunity to discuss this problem with a mixed group of military and civilian employees at a New England Air Force Installation. A colonel commented, "One of the greatest problems of employment — whether it is in industry or the military — is that we so much overestimate people's motivation toward progress and promotion that we gear all of our policies and procedures exclusively along these lines. Actually this leaves little provision for the guy who likes his job, enjoys his work, wants to continue at it.

"By way of example, I am an engineer because I like engineering. I didn't select engineering as a means to an end, or a step on the ladder, but as a profession which I enjoy, and to which I would like to dedicate myself. But the characteristics of promotion in the military services dictate that after satisfactory performance for a given period of time, I must be promoted. It means being promoted out of and away from what I enjoy most — and probably do best. But to refuse promotion would upset the applecart — and I would be forced into early retirement. So I have had to accept promotion and satisfy my engineering interests by taking a moonlighting job in engineering in whatever time off I have found available."

To understand the individual, as well as to provide for the utilization and fulfillment of his motivations, it is vitally important to know what he sees, seeks, and needs in his work. If emphasis is chiefly on promotion, this will actually have a tendency to *demoti*vate an individual whose interest is in the job itself. In effect, it's like telling him that his job is important only as a stepping-stone. What he *needs* to feel is that his job is worthwhile, and that his assignment to it is important and significant.

Personally I have great and equal respect for human effort toward progress — whether this progress is toward increased and diversified responsibility, or devoted to improving quality, skill, and output. And I have found it extremely helpful to think in terms of two kinds of promotion. The first is the traditional form of promotion, "up the ladder," which I call "vertical promotion." Furthering and refining of skills, enlargement of craftsmanship and work capacity are also progress — and I refer to this as "horizontal promotion."

As you may have noticed, this latter type of promotion does not refer only to non-supervisory jobs and craftsmanship. It also affects men and women who do an excellent job in front-line supervision, who have no interest or aptitude in more remote managerial assignments. Such individuals are promoted "horizontally" by enlarging the scope or volume of their responsibilities. If this terminology sounds trite or merely placating, remember that professionals — like doctors and dentists — measure *their* progress on the basis of "horizontal" rather than "vertical" promotion.

Not long ago a department manager in Taiwan asked how this philosophy could be put into practice with his non-skilled and semi-skilled workers, who, he felt, performed occupations in which there was not much potentiality for motivation. So I asked him if it were really important that the work be done. When he replied affirmatively, I next asked him if he would prefer to do the work himself. In the fact that he emphatically said that he would not, he showed that he placed both value and respect on the work and on the worker, and that he appreciated the worker, his efforts, and his accomplishments. As simple as this is, it is the beginning of the supervisory attitude and response which are vitally important in establishing values in jobs and efforts, and in motivating employees.

What your employees need to feel in your attitude toward them is that you respect them and their capacities, and appreciate their efforts. In providing this, you assist your people to achieve the much-needed and vitally motivating sense of *self*-value in *work*-value.

Job Relationships

You probably have found in observing your own staff that many of the social relationships among non-supervisory people originate or are initiated by work relationships. And as this is a motivation which is growing in importance, it perhaps would be worthwhile to use several illustrations of the various forms it takes, and how it works.

At the time when I interviewed Mary Anderson, she was 72 years of age; she had passed discretionary retirement age, reached the mandatory period, and had requested special consideration to allow her to continue at work. When I reminded her that the company's generous retirement plan would be more than sufficient to meet her needs, she said, "It isn't a matter of money. Even without the pension, I would never have need for money. It's a question of my human relationships."

Mrs. Anderson had joined the company after graduation from high school, worked two years until her marriage, returned to work at age 25 as the widowed mother of two boys. At the present time, her sons are university department chairmen — one in psychology, one in mathematics; she has several grandchildren and great grandchildren.

"When I came back to work, I needed the work and I needed the money — and I continued to need them until after my sons had graduated from college. But my job gave me something more than that. With two boys to raise, I didn't have much time for socializing. All of my friends have always been the people with whom I worked — mostly from my own department.

"Oh, my sons are good to me — and they frequently ask me to go to live with them. But they understand me when I tell them that they have their own lives and I have mine; that mine is here, this is where my friends are, this is where my interest and skills are. I belong here — and if I am compelled to retire, I won't belong anywhere!"

Most of us have many times seen the truth of the motivation specialists' finding that money has no positive motivational impact. Money inadequacies and pay inequities create morale problems or motivate people to seek security, adequacy, survival rates. But motivation cannot be bought. As a means to an end, money may sometimes assist in fulfilling non-work motivations of employees. For instance, a number of companies have found technical people resigning high-paid "pressure jobs" for lower-paced, lower-paid jobs as soon as school graduation of their children reduces their financial responsibilities.

When the money question is merely one of amount, instead of adequacy, and is "tested" against actual human motivation, the proof becomes all the more clear. A few years ago, for example, I had the opportunity to talk with Clem Hardesty, a machinist, who was working with a Vermont company which had paid a great deal of attention to its employee relations, but very little attention to its community public relations. In answer to a number of questions that I asked him about his job, he said, "I like my job, my work place, and the people with whom I work. I like the bosses. The management has always been very good to me, showed respect for me. You know, I have never once asked for any equipment which they have not quickly provided. My wage rate is better than that of most other men in town who are doing the same kind of work. My work area is well lighted, air conditioned, and extremely pleasant. I get cooperation from all those with whom I work. Yes, I like my job and I like the company. But I am quitting on Friday night."

When I asked why, he explained, "Although it is not justified, this company has a poor public image in this town. The result is that my wife and youngsters are always defending me among their friends because I work in a place that the public regards so poorly. My family are tired of it and so am I. The new job that I will be starting on Monday will pay me more than 15 percent less, and working conditions are by no means as good. But it has a better public image — and will give me a better social identity in this community."

Our two illustrations reflect two differing kinds of relationship motivations in work. Mrs. Anderson was motivated toward the direct relationship with other workers. Clem Hardesty, the Vermont machinist, was motivated toward a community status and image through his work relationship. Other people may, for example, find that their job establishes or enables motivating relationship with others in a professional field — such as a society or association. And some people are motivated in their work either by a managerial responsibility relationship in the job, or the prospect that such a relationship can be attained.

The supervisor-manager must, therefore, explore the specific motivational needs with which an employee faces his work. And, finding individually what these motivational needs consist of, it is essential for the supervisor to identify and clarify where these motivating prospects are, what they consist of, and how they can be attained by the employee. Actually, this is a very fundamental part of the activity of orienting an employee to his job and his work place, assignment, and responsibilities.

The importance which people place on and seek from their work relationships and identity was amusingly accented in an article written a couple of years ago by a millionaire playboy. He complained that his greatest problem was that, not having a job, he had no human identity and no foundation for basic human relationships. He said that invariably the first question he is asked in meeting new people is, "What do you do for a living? For whom do you work?" He concluded that people classify, and understand men and women primarily in terms of the job that they hold, the status and nature of their work, and the corporate or community relationships formed by their work.

My own grandson showed me how early in life people start to

identify each other and identify with each other in terms of occupations. During a visit, my son took a candid camera picture of me as I was washing the dishes. I thought no more about it until one time, four months later, I overheard my grandson explaining to a playmate, "My daddy works for Liberty Company, and my grandpa washes dishes in Connecticut."

Significance of Job Results

It would be difficult to find a case in which social contribution is so clearly and unquestionably a planned work motivation as was true in the case of Pete Hammond, the lavatory technician. However, it is obvious that this is the fundamental motivation for most doctors.

At Nalews, Inc, construction engineers — a New Hampshire-based firm which constructs industrial and municipal water reprocessing, sewage disposal, and water cleansing installations — it has been found that one of the primary motivations and interests of key personnel and workers alike is social contribution and ecological improvement. In an opinion poll, a high percentage of people indicated that they liked their jobs — but an even higher percent reflected that they liked and believed in the social contribution of their work.

Recognition of the motivation of individual employees toward social contribution, for example, provides a supervisor with a very clear point to delineate and emphasize in his communications and relationships with employees.

Determining and Understanding Motivation

Manual ladling of molten metal was one of the first occupations singled out for review by Pascal ("Pat") DeLiso, General Manager of Hampden Brass and Aluminum Company, in his company's effort to update operations and improve working environment and conditions. As Mr. DeLiso explained, "This was one of the most unattractive jobs in the company. It was hot, dirty, and presented a considerable physical strain to the man who had to lift and pour."

Known by his people as an executive with an unusual degree of sensitivity, reasonableness, and accessibility, Pat was immediately approached by a ladleman who requested that the job remain unchanged. Pat clearly and patiently outlined the reasons for the proposed change and emphasized that the ladleman would not lose income, might actually gain. The answer was quick and blunt, "Sure, it's a hot, hard job. But it's a *man's* job — and there aren't many guys who could do it!"

One company in Japan finds no difficulty in securing male candidates for certain occupations which are more difficult, less pleasant, and which pay no more than others, " . . . because they are regarded as being clearly and exclusively man's work."

Often the whole framework of a man's sense of security or status rests on what he feels that he can do which few other people can do.

What is the employee specifically seeking; what does he need? Until he knows the answer to this for every individual in his work force, the supervisor cannot hope to fully motivate his employees.

One great source of errors and problems is in our tendency either to project or to generalize with respect to motivation. We expect people's values to be pretty much in terms of our own valuations, and that people will be motivated by these values. Or we often try to estimate what people will value in terms of what we regard as logical and rational. Both of these approaches can lead to serious misunderstanding, difficulty, and disappointment.

One of the most dedicated union officers I have ever known was Frank Perry. At the time of our acquaintance, Frank was President of the Local of the International Brotherhood of Paper Makers at Champion-International Company in Lawrence, Massachusetts. Frank was a totally sincere person, with a fine keen mind, unusual perspective on any problems with which he was confronted, and a unique capacity for projecting and accurately pre-estimating employee reaction to virtually any personnel program which might be under consideration.

Because of Frank's unusual capacity in dealing with people and their problems, and because of his obvious and sincere dedication to people, I felt that he would contribute a great deal in any of a number of managerial occupations to which he might be assigned — and that his people interests would provide him with the necessary motivation and inspiration.

Frank was a roll trucker. He physically pushed rolls of unfinished paper on four-castered dollies to supply the raw stock for the finishing operation. Frank consistently refused promotion. The reason he gave was, "I don't want any more responsibility" — an excuse which was a little hard to believe in the light of the degree to which he accepted and fulfilled the responsibilities involved as president of the union.

Then one day I overheard Frank talking with some of the men in the plant about "physical condition." The truth was that Frank had an excellent physique for a man in his fifties — and he believed that the daily physical strain of the roll-trucking job would sustain his fine muscular condition. In his early career, Frank had had a more sedentary managerial job — and had had health problems. So his values — and, thereby, his motivations — had become more center-ed on physical considerations.

I made the mistake of interpreting Frank's potential motives in terms of my own concepts and goals. We were both highly inter-ested in people — so I thought that Frank would feel as I did in aspiring to increase the potential scope of his contributions to people.

Motivation = Employees' Values

The paper industry also taught me that it is precarious to judge or presume on the basis of what we personally regard as "logical" or "rational." To me the shift-rotating plan in this industry is illog-ical, irrational, and insupportable. Called "tour work," shifts rotate every one, two, or three weeks. Fatigue studies indicate that it re-quires six to seven weeks for a person to adjust to any one schedule of meals, sleep, and work hours. Thus, the tour work of the paper industry does not permit adjustment to the constantly changing work-sleep schedule.

Hearing my criticism, John W. Jordan, who was then Vice Presi-dent and Secretary of the Brown Company in Berlin, New Hamp-shire, suggested, "What you say sounds logical. But, after all, this is a matter of choice for the people involved. Check it out: if you find that they agree with you, the tour system can be changed."

An informal poll — conducted with the help of the Union — of the employees involved in this shift plan reflected that they em-phatically wanted to continue it. Their reasons were not just resis-tance to change, but were as logical and rational in their way as my arguments had been against the tour arrangement. For instance, tour work released younger and lower-seniority workers from con-tinual assignment to the night shift; rotation enabled married men to spend different periods of the day with their families; varied social and recreational activities were made possible by rotation — matters which would be seriously restricted under a straight-shift plan. And some suggested that it was easier to live with frequent rotations than it would be to adjust from six-or-seven week rotation, because "things become a habit in that length of time." As logical and rational as their reasons were, they were all points which I had failed to consider, matters which I had to discover by exploring with the people themselves the values which they find in their daily lives, work, and environment.

One day, in presenting an "in-company" lecture-seminar program, I got a little carried away in trying to illustrate and emphasize the need to explore values in terms of people themselves, in order to determine people's motivations. I wanted to illustrate that *anything* can be a value symbol, and that the values may differ radically from one circumstance to another or from one person to another. And so I said, "Anything — anything at all in the lives or environment of people — may have value significance and motivating stimulus for people. *Anything* — why, even the light bulbs!"

The quiet which followed my emphatic statement made me uneasy. So I finally asked, "What did I say that is wrong?" To which one member of the audience replied, "How did you know? How did you know that in this company if you are a non-supervisor you get a 40-watt bulb, a supervisor you get a 60-watt bulb, a manager a 100-watt bulb — and if you are an executive you get a 100-watt bulb and a window."

Whether this is true or if he was pulling my leg is unimportant; the vital fact is that we must recognize that motivational goals which we may regard as trivial may have a very real, significant, and justifiable value to the individuals involved. Take, for instance, the size and location of a man's office, his desk, the location of a man or a woman at a work bench. All of these things must be weighed in terms of what they mean to the people involved — and *not* what we may regard as rational or valuable.

As a group of supervisor-managers pointed out, motivational values change — and in some cases reverse and become opposite. The superintendent of a plant in Thailand explained, in a seminar, an approach he had utilized to reduce morning tardiness: by captioning the portrait of a late-arriving girl worker "Tardy Employee of the Week," and posting it conspicuously on the bulletin board, he had embarrassed the girls into more prompt attendance. The group talked about the valid cause of lateness and the possibility of altering work schedules to reduce employee commutation problems. But they also mentioned the potentially negative image that this practice might have on morale, attitude, and productivity — and the possibility that disciplinary effect could turn in a completely opposite direction if employees became defiant, re-captioned the posting "Pretty Girl of the Week," or otherwise commenced to regard it as an "honor roll."

By definition, motivation means "compelling reason." It reflects that something has a special value and meaning to an individual — sufficient to become a "compelling reason" or motivation. And values necessarily vary from region to region, circumstance to circumstance, person to person. Water skis would assuredly offer little interest or value to an Arctic Eskimo, and snowshoes have little practical and usable value for Floridians. Our values and compelling reasons are so individual that they vary widely even within families.

Understand the Motivation of Each Individual

One of the most fascinating aspects of studying an individual's motivations is the extent to which it is possible to measure the potential degree of a person's dedication by knowing a little bit about the intensity of his compelling reasons, and the values which he places on them. It is also interesting to review from how many different roots can spring the same occupational dedication. Pete Bassett is a successful and dedicated physician. When Pete was quite young, his father died from lung problems incurred by his work in a coal mine. Pete's primary interest is in lung disorders, and his motivation is to help people and improve their conditions. Jack Harrington is also an excellent and well-known physician; actually, medicine is the third professional area in which he has been outstandingly successful. His father was the town drunk in the village where Jack was born. Jack's motivation is toward social acceptability, status, and social contribution. Both Pete and Jack placed unusual value on their "compelling reasons" — and thus have achieved an unusual degree of success. Knowing these basic motivations, it is easy to understand why Pete turned down the job of medical chief of a large hospital — and why Jack readily accepted a similar position.

A great many managers have gained basic insight into the motivation, compulsions, and potentialities of their staff members by exploring and discussing ten areas relating to these people's backgrounds and interests.

1. What is the background of the individual in terms of:
   (a) occupation of the father
   (b) occupation or social activities of the mother
   (c) number of children in the family
   (d) age relation of individual to father and mother
   (e) age relation of individual to brothers and sisters
   (f) financial condition of the home
2. Do occupational and interest areas of the individual follow or significantly differ from those of parents, brothers, or sisters?
3. Did father or mother have strong opinions regarding the course of education and career of the individual? Were these opinions followed? Or, did education and career take a similar, parallel, or contrasting direction?
4. What are the occupational and non-occupational activities of the individual?
5. What are the chief interests of the individual? (And do these coincide more with occupation or with non-occupational activities?)
6. What interests the individual most in his current occupation?
7. What interests the individual least in his current occupation?
8. How does the individual visualize his work of the future? What are his ambitions and aspirations? Why were these particular goals selected?
9. How well do these goals fit the realities of the individual's abilities, training, education, potentialities?
10. What does the individual's wife or husband think of these aspirations?

Identify How Specific Motivations Can Be Fulfilled by or in Job

Charles Tracy is one of the most effective, sensitive, and well-liked personnel managers I have ever known. And yet in his early career, he literally wandered all over the map, occupationally. Part of his inconsistent occupational pattern was due to job problems of the period — but in greater degree, it was due to Charlie himself, and the fact that he had not found the proper niche for his motivations.

Charlie knew that he basically wanted to work with people and with human development. So he elected a teaching career. Probably because he had chosen high school as the grade level for teaching —

and because of the resulting need for a specific subject area — he selected accounting and business administration, because these and mathematics had been his strong points while he was in school.

When Charlie left teaching, his background in accounting led him first into plant accounting, and then into production planning and control. His work habits and his attitudes had made him immensely popular with his co-workers and his bosses. So when company management decided to implement its first formal program of personnel administration, Charlie was chosen to develop and direct it. Edgar Pitt, who was then Vice President and General Manager of the company, remarked, "It's a natural for Charlie — and he's a natural for the job. He is sensitive, fair, and equitable toward people; he is well liked. And this seems to fit ideally to his motivation toward social contribution, helping and developing people."

As much as Charlie contributes in and through his job, his personal life is also consistent with his motivation toward social contributions. He is heavily involved with community activities, his local school board, scouting. And his sense of responsibility toward the people and the community activities to which he has committed himself has made him refuse to leave and re-locate — even for the prospect of a considerably increased income.

Through the wisdom of a sensitive boss, this man was guided into the field in which his motivations became fully identified and could find their fulfillment.

Emphasize Importance of Job-Man-Performance Relationship

In the midst of a rather general conversation, a young engineer with whom I was sharing a seat on an eastbound transcontinental plane suddenly said, "You know, I'm a very lucky guy: I've got a very understanding wife and family." When I asked him what he meant, he explained, "I just resigned from a secure job with a good, large, international company, to take a job at less pay with a small company in upper New York State. Rather than making the decision myself, I talked it over with my family, and let them make the decision for me.

"I explained to them," he continued, "that my position with the large company was secure, that the small company and the job with it were a lot more risky. I explained that the opportunities for the future with the large company were much more clear and assured.

And I explained that there was little chance that I would ever be fired in the operation or could be 'buried and forgotten.'

"But I also explained that just as mistakes and errors would not show up readily in the large company, neither would successes and accomplishments. My teen-aged son sort of clinched the decision when he said, 'Gee, dad, that's like working in a vacuum. What fun is there in working like crazy when your efforts and accomplishments don't show up — when no one recognizes them and the operation is so big that they don't show up? I should think that it would be awfully hard on someone who was really interested in his work!'"

Emphasize Values to Sustain Motivation

It is vitally important to remember that motivated effort is a form of human communication and must be treated as an inter-human experience. In our efforts to motivate people, we try to demonstrate the value of an occupation or activity, and the importance of a staff member's performance in that occupation. One member of a workshop on leadership remarked, "Sure, we're motivated — because we've got a good boss. He makes us feel that our occupations are meaningful and worthwhile, and that we're making an important contribution by doing them well." A second member of the same group added, "After all, the true value that you feel in a job and how you do it is what you feel in the boss' attitude toward the job and toward you. And I don't mean in the orientation spiel — I mean on a day-in-day-out basis."

The spokesman for a group of supervisors participating in a workshop on human behavior and supervision suggested, "Knowledge of individual motivations is a vital first step — and these must be identified, oriented, and directed. But a manager's responsibility does not stop there. Motivation is basically a matter of values, and values must be continually demonstrated and reaffirmed. The most skilled and motivated guy in your work force cannot continually proceed on his own steam; he's got to see the values that you have said are in the job and in his performance demonstrated also by your later acts and attitudes. This does not merely mean that he should be commended when he does the job well — equally, he should be disciplined when he does *not* do the job well. Whether it is in commending or disciplining, your attention, as well as the emphasis you give by follow-up, demonstrate your continuing belief in the importance of the job, of the man in it, and of his effort."

Or, as construction superintendent Nick Skrepnek commented,

"It is demoralizing to a man to be kept in a job once its value has diminished or disappeared — or it appears to have disappeared because of your lack of attention and concern. Lack of value or purpose for his effort is extremely hard on a man. Furthermore, to ignore or to fail to notice poor or inadequate work is hard on a man, as well as being hard on the job. When you let a man get by with poor or inadequate work, you take something away from him, make it apparent to him that his work is not important enough to be noticed. Or, when you fail to recognize and comment on work well done, you *also* take away from the importance of a man's job and of his effort."

A great deal of what we must do to sustain the motivation, efforts, and interests of people is indicated by the word "need." If we need something, it has value: if we do not need it, it does not have value. If we do not need a man's skills and motivations — or if our lack of interest makes it appear that we do not — the staff member inevitably feels a lack of value in his skills and efforts, and a lack of self-worth within himself. I have heard it expressed by more than one supervisor in the simplest terms, "If you need a man, appreciate him; if you don't need him, transfer him or release him."

If we need something, we will value and seek it. For instance, if we need an occupation to be done skillfully, we will value good performance, or we will insist that those who perform poorly improve until they provide us the results which we need. The results of following these simple rules inevitably exceed a manager's expectations.

On a late flight from Chicago to New York, only two seats remained when two late-arriving men boarded the plane; one of these seats was next to me, the other was across the aisle from it. As it turned out, the man who took the seat next to me was the recently appointed European sales manager of a large international hotel chain, and the other gentleman had been departmental assistant for a number of years.

A range of mutual interest made my conversation with the sales manager quite absorbing. Nevertheless, he noticed several times that his assistant across the aisle coughed rather heavily. Finally, he looked across the aisle, and asked, "Say, John, what's with this cough?" "Oh, I don't know, I've had it for six or eight weeks. It seems to hang on." "Have you seen a doctor?" "Oh, no — it will go away in time."

The sales manager looked at his assistant intently, "John, when we get to New York, I want you to see a doctor. You've got to get this thing cleared up! I need you." The assistant looked almost startled as he asked, "What was that you said?" The sales manager repeated, "We've got to get this thing cleared up — I need you." The assistant paused for a moment; finally he said, "You know, Walt, I've been with this company for over ten years — and that's the first time anyone has said anything like that to me!"

A few years ago, a Massachusetts electronics firm was so plagued with shortages of engineers and technicians that it offered all kinds of employment inducements and benefits to these technical people. Unfortunately, the pressure of this problem diverted their attention away from the problems, responses, and morale of workers in other occupations. Productivity and the general employment situation among production personnel gradually worsened to a point at which it was impossible for production departments to keep pace with engineering and technical developments and output.

A quick look at employment statistics showed that turnover among bench personnel, assemblers, and general operators had reached 108 percent per annum. Interviews with selected newcomers and long-term employees reflected their feeling that they were neglected, ignored, minimized. Their job and work attitudes had reached such a low ebb that quality control was impossible to maintain.

In a very real sense, the value of these workers was demonstrated and affirmed by the critical situation caused by their demotivation, disinterest, and turnover. So it was with complete and renewed sincerity that the general manager sent a letter to the homes of all production personnel, outlining certain new steps, provisions, and policies that the company had adopted, and ending up with a note, "Bear with us — we need you." In a period of less than four months, turnover dropped from 108 percent to 6 percent per annum, productivity reached its highest level in company history, and rejects and customer returns dropped by 40 percent.

The supervisor-manager who momentarily pauses, from time to time, to think about the severe and insurmountable pressures which would confront him if his work people suddenly were not available, finds himself viewing his employees and their efforts with renewed, positive appreciation. Like the feelings he expresses negatively when his people are absent and non-productive, he reflects positively toward them, their attendance, and efforts — "We need you."

9

PUTTING YOUR "PEOPLE POTENTIAL" TO WORK

When I was quite young, my father once upset my entire family by selecting as contractor a man who was known for low-quality, corner-cutting work, to do some construction on which my father wanted and expected an excellent job. When I questioned the wisdom of his choice, my father explained his thoughts: "It's true that this man has a reputation for shoddy work. And because of this reputation people seek him out only for work which they intend to be of low or marginal quality. For this reason he has no opportunity to show his skills on good quality projects. However, I've seen some of his workmanship, and have found some wonderful ideas and some excellent craftsmanship. He knows what I want. I've made it clear to him that I expect top-quality work, and that I'm going to see to it that I get it. This is an opportunity for him to demonstrate his craftsmanship, and to take pride in his work — and I am somehow certain that this is what he will produce."

When the project was completed, my father's expectations, confidence, and quality standards were superbly met: the building was truly a monument to the contractor who had built it. My father's explanation was: "A man can be no more, or produce no more, than the confidence, attitude, and expectations you extend to him. By looking for the negative in a man, you'll never allow him to show his positive side; you will necessarily get negative results. If you expect a man to be wrong, he can never really be right." In this instance, as in many others, my father demonstrated that he sensitive-

171

ly recognized people's potential, and understood people well enough to put that potential to work.

A supervisor's capacity to attain the highest degree of employee motivation and accomplishment depends on three things:

1. Recognition and assessment of people's potential: his ability to uncover, see, and visually project the potentialities of people.
2. Activation and direction of people's potential: the supervisor's potentiality *with* people — his ability to develop and stimulate people, and to activate and direct their potentialities.
3. Utilization and fulfillment: his capacity to assist people in attaining their potential — both in terms of resulting work and accomplishment, and in the satisfaction, fulfillment, and self-realization which they thereby obtain.

Recognition and Assessment

At the close of a seminar in Boston, a young supervisor privately asked me if I would administer tests to one of his workers. Asked why, he said: "This is a guy in whom I see tremendous potential. If I could get him started — could make him begin to realize his potential — I firmly believe that he would go on to become extremely valuable to himself and to other people. But I've spoken to him about this so often that he's formed the habit of brushing me off with the remark, 'That's just your opinion.' I need something in addition to my own opinion with which to convince him. In my bones, I feel that once he realizes just a bit of it, he'll go on like a house-afire. He's got a lot of energy, dedication, and a good head of steam for doing anything and everything which he feels confident that he can do."

To the experienced supervisor — or to anyone else who is sensitively aware of people — the most continual and dynamic lesson learned is that of the infinite and untapped resources of the potentiality of people. We are learning this more now than we ever did in the past, because our traditional management methods had the effect of minimizing and stifling people potential. In the past, management characteristically tended to assess people in terms of calculated risk rather than *potentiality*: in other words, to try to see what was actually or potentially *wrong* in individuals, rather than what is right. Yet if we look at the field of human development realistically, we realize that it consists of building on the potentialities of people. Such development cannot be based on negativism — or what is *wrong* with people.

What We Look For in People

Because accurate assessment of people's potentials demands that we develop comprehensive understanding of each individual employee — and, therefore, that we be as searching now in our positive efforts as we were in the past with our negative and protectionist efforts — the difference between historic and current human relations concepts is not always clearly apparent.

Many of the same interviewing techniques and questions are still used. But they differ fundamentally in the purpose for which the information is sought, and the way in which it is interpreted, understood, and utilized. For instance, one application form designed 30 years or more ago, included a series of illustrative questions: "1. Do you have diabetes? 2. Have you ever had any traces or symptoms of diabetes? 3. Has your father or mother ever had diabetes? 4. To the best of your knowledge, have any members of your family — brothers, sisters, aunts, uncles, or grandparents — ever had diabetes?"

The purpose of these questions was to explore and calculate the risk of employing an individual. It was thought that if other family members had had the disability, the risk was greater that it might develop in this individual. And if it did develop, the individual would become a greater hazard through the possibility of seizure, or his vulnerability to blood problems and disorders. Thus, such an individual was classified as "less desirable" than one who did not have such a precarious heritage. In the very truest sense, this was personnel selection through exploring the negative potential of people, rather than the positive potential.

Look Beneath the Surface

We still need to know a great deal about people, but we need to know in order to understand, develop, and motivate them, rather than to eliminate them. The "dossier of facts" indicated that Jim Hunter was a maverick. He was defiant and rebellious — and had served time for one of his escapades. He himself used minor drugs, and he vehemently expressed the belief that they should be legalized and made generally available. Jim had been summarily fired from his previous job "for insubordination."

Closer examination showed that Jim's "insubordination" had been his refusal to submit to a foreman's demand that he get a haircut. His use and support of marijuana was as an alternate or substitute for alcohol, which a tragic memory of his alcoholic father had made him despise and fear. His jail sentence was a result of a momentary association with a militant group, and his defiant refusal to exonerate himself of responsibility for vandalism which the group had previously committed and in which he had not been involved. His high school records showed that Jim had an extremely high I.Q. and that his grades had all been either high or low, with none in between.

Through interview questions, the supervisor found that the grades varied by teacher attitude, rather than by subject. When teachers mandated and required study, Jim's marks were low. Teachers who "were interested and interesting" brought out not only the subject-interest, but also a desire to please; in such cases, Jim's grades were extremely high.

Looking at the "why" instead of at the mere facts themselves, the interviewing supervisor saw in Jim an intense personal need for relating to people and being useful to them. So he assigned him as "trainer" for the department. With his excellent mind stimulated by the potentiality for being useful to people, Jim learned all of the occupations of the department quickly, thoroughly, and well. What made him especially effective as a trainer was his capacity to see an occupation as trainees would see it, and to provide in advance full and satisfactory answers for all of their questions.

Accuracy and Sincerity Are Essential

A young boy who was periodically trounced by one of his classmates noticed in a novelty store a gadget on which the label read "Strengthen yourself by purifying your blood." The machine consisted of two electrical conductor knobs. When both the knobs were simultaneously held, and the one on the right was turned clockwise, increasing voltage up to a safe maximum was allowed to pass through the circuit.

Reading this, the boy accepted it with complete trust. He converted his allowance into the coins required by the machine. And for the next three days, he repeatedly operated the machine to its maximum. On the fourth day, with new-found self-confidence, he assaulted the bully — and again was knocked flat on his back. A person's acceptance of confidence in himself is an expression of trust in the agent by which the confidence is given. And it is a devastating thing to discover that the confidence has been inaccurate, insupportable, or artificial.

As we have discussed in various sections of this book, people's motivations are changing, and these and their identification needs are becoming more and more associated with occupations, occupational and work relationships, and social contribution through work and effort. In direct ratio to this shift into work, the immediate supervisor becomes increasingly important to the individual employee. The more work-related motivations, identification, and self-worth become, the more important the supervisor becomes as a source of the fruition and fulfillment of these individual human needs.

The position of the supervisor is thus increasingly vital to the employee, as it is also to the company: this is the only position from which human assets can be sensitively determined, as well as activated and made productive. To the employee, the supervisor necessarily is an authority on the content, value, and prospects of an occupation, its performance, and its rewards. Thus, to the employee, the supervisor is also a visionary by whom individual ability, capacity, and potential must be seen, planned, developed, assigned, and promoted. To the average employee, his "immediate boss" is the only one who can sufficiently understand him and his potential and, at the same time, know the prospects and channels for progress. "The boss" is thereby the only one who can fit the two together productively for mutual benefit.

What a Worker Needs and Looks For

A basic characteristic of humanness and sociability relates us to our job and to other people in a way that directly pertains to the responsibility of the supervisory manager. The fact that we are "social animals" means that we are fundamentally impelled toward relationships and relating. And so a major part of our continual assessment of the world around us is an effort to determine how we relate to the persons, environments, or situations by which we are confronted. In terms of work, work-motivation, prospects, this means that we try to understand the work and work environment in terms of ourselves, to see how we fit them, and how and what they specifically mean to us.

Being acutely aware of the fact that there are many aspects and ramifications of the work and environment about which we do not know — and also of ourselves as we potentially fit to the current and future requirements of the work and its environment — we necessarily seek guidance in our thinking. Our immediate supervisor invariably becomes the source of such advice, guidance, and development. This is true not only because of the influential role which such a supervisor plays in determining and deciding our work futures, and his close knowledge of the requirements of the job and work place, but also because of his knowledge and proximity to us, and his capacity thus to visualize our capabilities being used now and in the future.

The supervisor who fails to provide this vision and guidance — either through neglect or inability — leaves a serious gap of unfulfilled need in his subordinates. His people have no alternative source: no one else has the combined people-and-occupation knowledge to answer this need. Yet it must be done with the utmost of thoughtfulness, sensitivity, accuracy. It is a tragic thing to mislead people into false confidence or expectancy, whether it is done by error or by intent. And it is equally unfair to perpetuate an employee's ill-founded or unsupportable hope, anticipation, or expectancy.

The so-called "Peter Principle" suggests that all people sooner or later are promoted to their level of incompetence. And there is a great deal of truth in this contention. However, it reflects that the immediate supervisors of the people to whom this happens, who have "reached their level of incompetence," have failed in their jobs and in their responsibilities.

It goes without saying that a supervisor with real operational expertise precisely matches together occupational requirements and human capacities. So when workers have been promoted to their level of incompetence, it is obvious that their supervisors have somehow failed them. But even more important, it reflects that the supervisor did not possess or practice enough people potential to accurately define, develop, and relate his people to the occupations for which they had valid potential and competence. Whether it is in the encouragement of confidence and development, or in the clarification of the limits of employees' potentialities, there is an equal demand for the supervisor's sensitivity, concern, and accuracy.

Activation and Direction of People's Potential

A Denver-area supervisor, describing his experience in working with craftsmen from one of the American Indian nations, suggested,

"These people have taught me a lot about myself and about people whom I thought I knew and understood. Like most supervisors, I have a lot of little latitudes which I keep and use as incentives and work stimulants — such things as special time off, extra overtime, raises, promotion prospects, and the like. And I always thought that at least one of these would appeal to almost anyone. But I came a cropper with the Indian people; they taught me a lot about incentive values — and they taught me clearly and quickly."

He went on to explain that several in this group had particularly outstanding potential. He had tried raises, promotions, and every incentive he could think of to interest them in developing their potential. Nothing seemed to have any helpful impact. Then one day one of these men approached him with a request for three days off for himself and a group of others; he mentioned that his tribe was holding some sort of ceremony in which all of them wished to participate. Partly because he was irritated at their prior failure to respond to his suggestions and requests, and partly because he felt that his department could not function with such a large group absent on three regularly scheduled workdays, the supervisor refused permission.

Nothing more was said. But on the day that the ceremony was scheduled to start, the entire group was missing; similarly, on the next two days the group was still absent; on the fourth day, all of them were back at work, acting as if nothing had happened. So he called in the man who had originally made the request, confronted him with the fact that they had stayed out without permission, and mentioned his exasperation about the ignoring of prior suggestions regarding their development potential.

The employee looked at him fixedly and rather pointedly reminded him that incentives must be in terms of what people want, need, or value — and this is something that differs not only from people to people, but from man to man. The ceremony had been important to the men, and thus could have been an incentive; but instead, the way the supervisor had handled it had made it a challenge between his authority and their values and determinations.

"But let me give you some advice about what you think are stimulants and incentives," the employee continued. "Promotion? none of us want that. We like what we're doing, we do it well, and we like working together; we don't want to be separated either by promotion or change of occupation. Money? we're all making enough so that we are not much concerned about it, and if we don't earn it here, we can get similar jobs at equal pay somewhere else. Time off for extra vacation? Free time is an incentive only when it enables you to do something you value doing at a time when you want to do it. These three days were an incentive to us — but because of the way you reacted to our request, it was an incentive for us to challenge or ignore your authority, rather than the incentive it could have been to do something constructive or additional in our work."

In other words, the prospect of fulfilling his potential must be value-related for the employee — and this value must be his own assessment of what is important to him or for him. He must either have direct interest in what can be achieved through the development of his potential, or he must be interested in the effect or usefulness of the status he can thereby receive. Even in the matter of personal development, progress, promotion — factors which we are erroneously inclined to believe are attractive and stimulating to all people — it is necessary to understand how they fit the *workers'* values and motivations, not how they might fit our own.

Relating Workers' Potentialities to Their "Values"

Lars Johanson was made shop steward in a medium-sized electrical assembly plant. In this position he was more "visible" to management, so they became aware of the sensitivity, fairness, wisdom, and judgment with which he handled the problems in which he became involved. And he did excellent work in his regularly assigned occupation. To all suggestions that he either accept a management position or utilize his considerable accumulated seniority to bid off on a higher-paying job, he consistently replied that he was comfortable, contented, and happy in his work.

Friction arose when another shop steward publicly called Lars a "pro-management dupe" in relation to a case which Lars had actually handled with fairness, sound judgment, and expertise — and to the complete satisfaction of both the union membership and the management. Although Lars immediately resigned his stewardship, nothing more appeared on the surface for several months. Then, an hour before the 72-hour closing time on a vacancy for which only Lars' adversary had bid, Lars exercised his greater seniority and took the job.

It was thereafter discovered that for all the intervening period, Lars had carefully watched the vacancy list, and whenever his adversary's name appeared on the list, Lars persuaded someone with greater seniority to place and win the bid. When Lars later became personnel director of the plant in which he had been shop steward, he commented, "It takes a lot of different kinds of things to get a guy going. Bob and I are close friends now; whether or not he intended it, he gave me the boot in the pants it took to make me crawl out of my comfortable rut. And I must admit that I feel a greater sense of self-worth and fulfillment in my job — and I don't mind the responsibility nearly as much as I expected to."

The Thought Applies to Many People

The dean of a southern college called a mediocre student to his office. After discussing the student's lackadaisical attitude and poor marks, he concluded, "So I called you here to suggest that you drop out of college. You're not interested in much of anything — and it's a shame to waste your father's money under these circumstances. But that wouldn't be so bad . . . ." And the dean carefully and meticulously drew a verbal picture of the "very attractive future" which awaited the student after his college resignation — all glowingly painted in terms of what he specifically knew the student would find unthinkable and impossible. Eighteen months later, he again summoned the student from class; grinning at him, the dean said, "Congratulations on your excellent progress and average during these past few months. But it really goes to prove that you really can't 'turn on' some people until you make them mad, can you?" (He transferred shortly after our conference, so I've never had a chance to adequately thank him for his wisdom, understanding, and help.)

Accent the Worker's Positives

Strategies pertaining to the kindling of employee response and potential remind me of two classic books and a famous play. In his book *How to Win Friends and Influence People,* Dale Carnegie suggested the potent stimulus of focusing thoughts and conclusions directly on people themselves, patterning our conversation closely to them and to their interests. This tactic pays off well not only in discovering what we need to know and understand about people, but also in creating in them the responsiveness stimulated by the feeling of our interest and concern.

Norman Vincent Peale's book *The Power of Positive Thinking* (and its sequel, *The Amazing Results of Positive Thinking*) reflect the attitude and tone which discover and stimulate the potential of people. Not only is positivism an attitude and stimulation of growth, but it also indicates greater concern for the achievement of people potential than the stifling and dwarfing negativism of preoccupation with risk prevention.

And the play, *Promises, Promises,* suggests a vein or interpretation which these explorations and discussions must carefully avoid. The promises of a man's potentialities are promises which he must himself fulfill. The over-zealous supervisor often finds that an employee interprets promises as guarantees made to him by the supervisor, rather than requirements for dedication and effort on his own part.

As one experienced supervisor meticulously phrased it to a young worker whom he was counseling, "Steve, a man's potentialities are more a self-assurance than a promise; they indicate what you *can* do, if you *will* do it. Potentialities actually are a demand on a man; they are a reflection of what a man must do, must accomplish, in order to attain his sense of well-being, achievement, and self-worth. They are the promise which a man must make to himself, and must fulfill for himself. It's your life, and it's your decision — but let me tell you something: what I've learned from years of knowing and watching people in their work is that the *only* way a man can attain happiness, well-being, peace, and a sense of fulfillment is to know what his potential is, and to dedicate himself to attaining it, no matter what it is and what it requires. People who are unwilling to do whatever is necessary to achieve their potentials — or refuse to accept what their potentialities suit them for — are restless and unhappy people, because they live with a constant feeling of the unfulfilled promise of their lives."

Relating People to Their Potential

Once we have clearly and accurately assessed an employee's potential, and have found that we are sincerely able to identify this with current and future prospects of work and occupation, it is essential next to discover the extent to which these potentialities and possibilities hold value and incentive for the employee himself. Some of this, of course, can be readily discovered by comparing the employee's potentialities with his aspirations and motivations. And an even more reliable indication can be gained by determining how these potentialities and possibilities promise to measure up and fulfill the self-image of the individual.

Bearing in mind that people potential depends only partly on mental and physical capacity — and must be supported by employee response, willingness, and interest — the nature of a supervisor's explorations and efforts becomes more distinct. The simplest cases are those in which all four factors of interest, capability, motivational identification, and self-image totally coincide. For instance, when an employee's abilities are in the field of engineering, his interests are in scientific, computational, and, possibly, mechanical subjects. When he prefers to work by himself and is relatively low in sociability ratings, regarding his circumstance as happiest when he is in a position of respect but little responsibility for interaction with others, he will be stimulated by his own potentialities and possibilities in the field of engineering research, evaluation, and non-supervisory status.

The most forceful combination is when the abilities and interests are directly related, as they are in this particular case. But in our earlier discussion of the interests which lead a man or woman into the practice of medicine and thereafter support success in that profession, we noted how many and varied interests may suitably guide a person toward the same occupational choice. In our study of Pete and his work and motivations, we reflected how a man may find fulfillment of interests and motivations through performing an occupation which has no direct or technical correlation to the work itself. A study of the interest patterns of a group of very capable and effective construction superintendents surprisingly indicated a relatively low interest in scientific, statistical, engineering, or mechanical subjects, but a significant and fairly uniform interest in art and artistic activities. From this, we might conclude that at least a measure of the work interest and work gratification of these men pertains to the symmetry, design, and balance of the structures and grounds which they are assigned to construct.

Relating Aims to Potentials

On the one hand, the correlation of interest and occupational content or status is often surprising. It is amazing how some facets or features of a job may become emphasized and expanded or interpreted to fulfill the superficially unrelated interest and value needs of workers. But on the other hand, a large measure of a supervisor's effectiveness in stimulating people toward the fulfillment of their potentialities rests, first, in his capacity to recognize and visualize these potentials, and second in his ability to sincerely, clearly, rationally, and supportably identify the fruition of these potentials — and of employee interests and motivations — in the job content, job relationships, or job contribution.

A great deal of the latent force which a sensitive supervisor can generate in activating, applying, and fulfilling his people potential centers at just this point in his explorations, planning, and communication. You will find that it thus justifies thoughtful review of a variety of related considerations:

1. Is the employee's potential something of which he was previously fully aware?
2. How does the employee's potential compare with his self-assessment of his potentialities?

   In nature: is it in the same subject, occupational, or professional field?

   In extent: does his self-expectancy of growth or progress exceed or minimize his actual prospects?

   In degree: how does the stature of the occupation and of the possible place of the employee within it compare with his anticipations?
3. Does he concur with your assessment of his potentialities — in nature, extent, and degree?
4. How does his selection of occupation compare with his basic pattern of interests?

   Is it directly related?

   Is it geared primarily to by-products, such as fulfillment of a desire to contribute through the products or results of his efforts?

   Does it imply satisfaction through a role, status, or professional image?

   To what extent will the assignment, job content, work relationships, and work products and accomplishments meet and fulfill his primary major positive interest?

   Does his life style (social and recreational patterns) provide for expression and exercise of major interests not included in the occupation?

   To what extent are his negative interests necessarily and importantly included in current and anticipated occupations?
5. What is the occupation of his father? Mother?

   How does this compare and coincide with his occupational elective?

How does the social position of the work toward which he aspires — and for which he has capacity — compare with that of his parents? Other members of his family?

How does the income potential of his selected career pattern compare with that of his parents?

6. To what extent does he reflect comparability or dissimilarity from the domestic patterns and tastes of his early home life?

7. To what extent does he recognize and accept the need for self-dedication in the development of his potential? Or, conversely, to what extent does he give this secondary consideration and apply his priorities to more immediate personal, domestic, or social problems?

8. What is the elapsed time involvement and nature of development he will require to fulfill his potential?
   a) Job experience only.
   b) On-job training.
   c) Company-sponsored training adjuncts.
   d) Some outside institutional courses.
   e) Technical or general college-level credit courses during non-working hours.
   f) Leave of absence for added academic qualifications.

9. To what extent does he have initiative and drive? Is he a self-starter?

10. Will the pattern of assigned occupation and the development program enable you to provide surveillance, interest-stimulation, and vitality?

Securing Mutual Understanding of Your Subordinate's Potential

The idea that occupations are the principal basis of human identity and identification is by no means new. In the earliest of cultures, the particular skills with which a man contributed to the well-being of the tribe or community were the basis on which his identity was formed. Many widespread family names reflect this: for example, Sawyer, Goldsmith, Smith, Miller, Farmer, Fisher. In actuality, the current increase in importance of the role of occupations in human identity and as a source of motivational response and fulfillment is a restoration, rather than a new development.

However, the vital degree to which occupations have become the principal resource for fulfillment of motivational and identity needs does emphasize both the importance to the individual and the essential role which the supervisor has in directionalizing of occupational development, interests, and efforts. And it reveals, too, the extreme to which wisdom, thought, and accuracy are requisite. It is an area of personal career planning in which the average man or woman needs assistance, perspective, sensitivity, understanding, and confidence.

George Nixon had recently acquired his M.B.A. degree when he personally sought to explore and re-evaluate his own direction of maximum potential, and the specific practical steps which should be followed in attaining it. "I know what subjects I'm most interested in — and I think this is evident in my grades," he commented. "But I can't confidently say that I know what pattern of interest this reflects — and I most assuredly don't know what it means in the world of occupations. For these past several years, I have spent my time studying and learning. But there is a considerable difference between learning and applying, between studying and practicing. I need to know more about industries in general, how they differ, and what each has to offer. And I need to clarify what my interest patterns mean before I can wisely select an appropriate career pattern and the interim steps which are appropriate for working toward that goal."

George took a series of psychological tests with which it was possible to visually review his whole range of interests and personality traits in perspective. He felt that he needed this to judge what he should seek in his subsequent exploration of occupational prospects — contents and natures and the environmental factors of work. Thereafter, he visited a series of companies and institutions which were carefully selected to give him a wide diversity of industry type and size. Then, armed with information about himself and about occupational characteristics — and the strength and the self-confidence given him by the advice and responsive reception he had received from all the executives and officers with whom he had visited — George made a wise selection of the job and training to which he had become committed.

What George had done for himself, the majority of workers need to have done for them by their supervisory leaders. The perspective on himself — interests, personality needs and natures, capacities, and potential capabilities — which George had sought through review of his academic records and the indication of psychological tests, for most people must come from the sensitive observation, analysis, and "people potential" capability of "the boss." And the content, requirements, and environmental circumstances of occupations, which George had sought broadly and specifically from seasoned executives in a variety of industries, enterprises, and corporate situations, each worker needs to find and obtain through the guidance and suggestions of his supervisor.

Communicating and Mutualizing
Your People Potential

As the experienced supervisor becomes sensitively aware of the magnitude and importance of his human and operational responsibilities in determining and activating his people potential, he becomes more and more concerned about the accuracy and adequacy of his judgment. So he tends to become more deliberate, sensitive, and cautious — and to assure himself that he has considered every aspect, facet, and data source.

"There are so darned many things which you must consider which you ordinarily don't know about a man — and have no way of knowing — that I don't see how you can do an accurate job of it without making it a mutual study, with the employee himself," an Indiana-based unit manager remarked. "After all, it's a mutual interest of the company and the man himself — if it's right for him, it's right for the company, and vice versa. So what I try to do is to guide these conferences with employees, rather than to be dictatorial or decisive. I try to provide him with projective analysis and whatever counsel I can from my own experience and observation. He has to make his own decision but I try to provide him with some of the things he needs to make his decision wisely."

As advance homework, this supervisor studies a worker's background, training, interest, and motivations, and compares these with the various suitable occupations and programs of the company. Then, in conference with the individual, he uses some tentative thoughts as guidelines, illustrations, and thought-stimulants for the worker. Through questions and suggestions he stimulates the worker, gets him "in on the act"; together they work out a real mutual understanding — and, very often, a very clear and comprehensive long-range program of work and development is set up. His cautious tentativeness is very wise, because it is surprising how many bits of information and angles you learn in the course of these conferences, things which you didn't previously know, or hadn't even thought about, but that are vitally inportant in formulating a suitable and stimulating program for the worker.

"My own original boss did this for me, when I first joined the company," he continued. "That was 14 years ago; I had graduated from high school, but had no skills — I had worked only as an attendant in a filling station. The boss seemed to feel that I had potentialities I didn't know about, and fields that I hadn't even thought about. The fact that he knew what he was talking about seems pretty clear in the light of the fact that I'm still here, and that I'm increasingly happy in my work." The supervisor had recently earned his master's degree in electrical engineering, through a company-sponsored program of off-hours training and education.

The Infinite Prospect of Your People Potential

The supervisor-manager with sensitive capacity in the sphere of people potential discovers the degree to which people can exceed the limits of their own self-estimates, and is thereby able to guide them toward the attainment of unexpected accomplishment — to the extreme benefit of operations. In full exercise of people potential — what we can accomplish *with* and *through* people — it necessarily follows that there is a sizable portion of what we can do *for* people, in helping them to discover and attain their potentialities.

Securing mutual understanding of your subordinate's potential is not difficult when you are reasonably accurate and are flexible in your initial ideas, and when you provide employees adequate time and demonstration upon which to develop confidence in your interest and in your knowledge. The most difficult cases are those in which the worker either overestimates or underestimates his potential. But even these problems can be readily resolved when adequate time, thought, and understanding are devoted to the employee's concepts, reasons, and point of view.

During World War II, Navy Lieutenant Sabol patiently and consistently tried to convince and "bring out" a reticent young officer, who the Lieutenant believed had high people potential. Extremely competent and well-informed on military tactics, maneuvers, theory, seamanship, the young officer retreated into his shell like a turtle, when it came time for him to communicate, instruct, and command.

Lieutenant Sabol finally contrived a situation in which the young officer was compelled to participate, without recourse to "I can't" or the opportunity to retreat into his shell. At a battalion formation, the Lieutenant arranged for all officers senior to the young officer to be absent, instructed three of the remaining young officers to apply pressure, and he himself failed to show up. Being the senior officer present, the young officer had responsibility for the formation and report — a confrontation which the cohorts in the experiment made clear, and in which they encouraged him. When Lieutenant Sabol arrived at the scene ten minutes later, he was rewarded by finding his experiment totally successful, and the young officer went on to become a strong and effective leader.

Many times I have heard of similarly contrived solutions in industry — supervisors being intentionally absent from an area at a time which required and impelled action on the part of a qualified but self-minimizing employee. As one supervisor commented, "Look, we used participation as a training device — we instruct, we get people to actually do something themselves. People learn by doing, and they gain self-confidence by doing. So why is this very different? After all, you are merely trying to persuade and stimulate a man to do what you already know he is fully able to do well."

10

DEVELOPING YOUR PEOPLE'S
TALENTS AND POTENTIALITIES

Bell Laboratories has one of the finest training programs that I have personally had the opportunity to review. After an initial period of job training and orientation, well-performing employees are given a wide range of choices of in-company or institutional and collegiate courses through which they can prepare and progress in their chosen fields of specialization. Morale and enthusiasm for the company run high.

Young people often tell me that they have chosen the companies by which they are employed "because it's a place where you can learn, grow, and progress." A young technician explained his enthusiasm for the company for which he worked by saying, "It's a place to learn — and to apply what you learn."

Conversely, I have talked with a number of young men and women who are dissatisfied with their employment because such potentialities as these do not exist in their companies. They regard "opportunity" as being progress in either promotion or the development of skills and self-values: when neither of these exists, they are disgruntled and apathetic; when both of them are available, morale and responsiveness almost invariably are high.

The Risks, Challenges, and Rewards
in Development Programs

The current rapid pace of change in business and industry has intensified corporate interest in training and development. This is true partly because of the resulting need for new skills; partly because involvement of people in the process of change diminishes their resistance and makes them more understanding, constructive and flexible toward change. It also is partly because the increasing "community conscience" of corporations makes it unwise or immoral to permit the widespread obsolescence layoffs which otherwise would be inevitable. A prolonged period of shortage in technical labor markets further influenced management toward a "do-it-yourself" concept of securing requisite employee skills through company training.

And finally, as a result of a high birth rate a couple of decades ago, the average age of Americans has dropped to 27 years, and the percentage of young people in the labor market has increased dramatically. Fringe benefits developed during the period of higher-age employees — chiefly centered in issues of security — provide little incentive or motivational impact to younger people, who are more concerned with more immediate issues and progress. In countless cases, education, training, and development provide a suitable and effective stimulating fringe benefit for the younger people.

New Types of "Fringes"

A small urban New England company in a highly competitive and marginal industry established a very liberal education and training program designed specifically to attract ambitious young workers and supervisors. Too small to support and administer a fully effective in-company development program, the firm worked out programs with local public schools, adult education courses, vocational and technical institutes, and colleges. For young people who were interested in furthering their education and training, life became a virtual work-study program: full work-schedules were maintained, but hours of work were adjusted to enable attendance at suitable courses; all successfully completed courses were subsidized by the company.

"We're too small and too financially pressured to compete with larger companies in either salary rates or long-range promotion potentialities," 24 year-old supervisor Alan Spaulding explained. "Yet we need young people — we need their interests, efforts, skills, and ideas. So we've intentionally set ourselves up to be a stepping stone for young men and women who have ideas and ambitions.

They usually outgrow us in two to four years; but while they're here, they do a h--- of a job for us!"

Make Suggestions — Not Promises

But unless it is clearly spelled out, defined, and limited, proposal of training and development implies a future promise to those who respond and cooperate. (Sometimes you have to be very careful to make sure that your workers don't think it's a promise which necessitates little effort on their part.)

"I'm frankly afraid to push the matter of training and development too far or too hard," Ken Simeone, plant production superintendent, remarked. "I want to; my company has been slow to adapt to change and I know that all of a sudden it's going to hit us hard, and find us unprepared. When that happens there will be a mad scramble to acquire new technical skills. Because personnel development cannot be accomplished overnight, it means that we will go outside to find the talents we need. Our own people and their skills will be obsoleted. But we're not currently moving ahead very fast — and I have no idea of our timetable for change — I cannot sincerely promise the availability of job promotion that is implied by efforts and programs of training and development."

In one Connecticut community, a training and development program was jointly sponsored by well-intentioned contributors and public funds for the purpose of preparing unemployed, unskilled, and semi-skilled local people to fill jobs available in the area. Needs of local industry were carefully surveyed, and appropriate training courses were designed and provided. Allowing for expected drop-outs, training was made available to a 25 percent higher number than the estimate of job vacancies.

By the time the trainees had completed their programs — 18 months later — 30 percent or more of the jobs had been filled, about 50 percent had been eliminated or obsoleted, some had changed, and approximately ten percent remained for consideration by the trainees. The situation was made all the more critical by the fact that the number of drop-outs was substantially below that expected, so that trained applicants exceeded the number of vacancies by a ratio of roughly 12 to one.

It doesn't take more than one or two experiences of this nature to make a man hostile, uncooperative, untrainable, and unemployable.

Analyzing the Foundations and Prospects for Development

One of the first preliminary actions in considering training and development programs, is to carefully and critically examine the potential and probable opportunities which can be offered on completion of the recommended training programs. To do this effectively, simultaneous consideration must be given to what a worker will learn and how he will develop in the experience of his regular occupation, during the period that he is undergoing supplementary training and education. For instance, what aspect of his current assignment can directly or indirectly prepare him for the vacancy for which he will then be considered?

The most reliable resource which is immediately and generally available is the job description for the occupation to which the worker is currently assigned. This represents a list of work activities and requirements in which the employee will gain experience and knowledge in the daily conduct of his work. So to this list should be added the subjects and skills which are being included in the training and development program in which the worker is participating.

Next, this amended list should be compared with the description or specifications for all of the promotion or alternative positions for which the worker may be eligible for consideration. This comparison should be made on a detailed item-by-item basis in order to determine, in relation to the potential new assignment, (a) the subjects or areas in which the worker will be fully qualified and full-functioning on the completion of his current training and development program; (b) the subjects or areas in which he will need additional or supplementary training and development — and an estimate of the time and availability of such training; and (c) what subjects and areas still will be lacking in the employee's experience and education. To ensure that this analysis includes all related data, the list should also be scanned in terms of any education and experience the worker may have had prior to his employment by the company.

Determining the Individual's Needs Accurately

This information is a vitally important prerequisite for any consideration or planning of an individual's appropriate development program. But as essential as it is, it still is only a preface. Next, the worker's performance, aptitudes, talents, interests, work habits, and work relationships must be reviewed in minute detail. If your company's employee appraisal form is comprehensive, detailed, and suitable, this can serve valuably in analyzing each individual's training and development needs. If it is not adequate or sufficient, a helpful form can easily be designed which will assist you in appraising and reviewing your people, as well as providing you an accurate analysis of their training and development requirements.

Sometimes I suggest to supervisors that the best time to design an appraisal and development form is on the third day of a four-day fishing trip. This is because fair, equitable, and accurate appraisal or diagnosis of workers' training needs demands perspective, comprehensiveness, and objectivity — and these three things must be "built in" to the form which is designed for this purpose. It thus should not be prepared while under pressure.

What *is* appraisal? It is the assessment of the extent to which an employee does his job and conducts himself in a manner suitable to his work place and his working relationships. In effect, it is a measurement of the degree to which the employee fulfills what is expected of him.

Thus, a very workable appraisal and training analysis device can easily be designed by merely listing specifically and inclusively all the things which you, the company, and the job expect and require of an employee. Do this in general terms, rather than those found in job instructions and specifications: for instance, instead of enumerating, "Rotate the right-hand thumbscrew three complete turns, counter-clockwise," phrase it more generally, "Make necessary machine adjustments." In this way, you will find that a single list can be made comprehensive and inclusive enough to be used in connection with all the occupations and personnel under your jurisdiction.

— A Potent Instrument of Many Uses

Once completed, this list can be useful to you in a number of ways, and can help immensely in building rapport with your workers. For example, *all* of your employees know that you expect them "to do their jobs," but how many of your people are sure that they know what you feel "doing the job" consists of? How many of your workers are sure that your expectations and requirements are consistent, uniform, and equitable? Since their rating, status, and well-being as employees depends primarily on your assessment of them, they need to know the things upon which your judgment and assessment are based — and thus, in effect, a clear list of these items serves as a guideline or goal for them to adopt and follow. So to show them this list which you have prepared both demonstrates the consistence and equitability of your judgment and provides you with greater support for what you ask of your subordinates.

If you were to use this checklist device you have designed in appraising the performance of your employees, you would review it item by item, and pick the five performance areas in which a worker is doing best, and the five areas in which he has the greatest and most pressing need for improvement and remedial action. This identical technique works similarly in analyzing the training and development needs of the individual. As a matter of fact, it is the most accurate and dependable analysis of individual training and development needs that you can attain by any method. After all, it represents and summarizes your observations and judgments, checked on an item-by-item basis, to conclude which, among all requirements, are the most crucial and pressing needs.

Be Realistic in Demands and Expectations

Incidentally, some supervisory managers have questioned why I suggest the selection of *five* items, when in many cases, as they reflect, more than five areas need significant development and improvement. Being realistic about it, it is very simple: with effort, an employee can improve and develop in five aspects of his job; he cannot reasonably be expected to improve in more than five areas all at once. To select five items puts the improvement and development goals within range of his capacities and capabilities, and thus encourages him. To select too many development areas for simultaneous improvement makes the prospect formidable and insurmountable to him, and he becomes discouraged, demoralized, and quits trying.

Properly and sensitively administered, this simple device yields the most accurate attainable analysis of training and development needs of the individual. Summarily — as all the individual analyses for the department are compiled together — it provides the most accurate analysis of the training development needs of your department as a whole.

Establishing a Constructive Foundation for Developing Your People Potential

There are no two phrases with which a supervisor can so rapidly disturb and deteriorate a man's self-confidence and equilibrium than by calling him "a good man" or "a bad [or inferior] man." Disregarding for the moment the fact that either phrase is inept and its use is unfair, the supervisor must concentrate on words and tones which more clearly indicate that he is talking about a man's performance and conduct, and not about his character.

Especially in small companies, supervisors develop a tendency to classify a worker as "a good man" without defining the specific area or nature of his excellence, and he remains somewhat on a pedestal until someone erroneously regards the "good" as an all-inclusive classification and transfers him into a job outside his realm of competence and capability — then suddenly the "good man" becomes a "bad man."

If you are going to do an effective job of training and developing people, you must develop the habit of concentrating your judgment and assessment on a worker's skills, talents, and performance — not on his character. And you must notice good and poor performance and capability with equal sensitivity and perspective. If you do this, you will ultimately attain a degree of easy and relaxed rapport with your workers in which private discussions regarding training and development needs and suggestions take on an atmosphere of dispassionate mutual planning sessions, in which the instruments of their skills and capabilities, rather than mechanical equipment, are being programmed for their optimum and most beneficial use.

There is nothing more destructive of a worker's self-confidence, aspiration, morale, sense of security, and self-worth than a supervisor's comment, "You're doing a lousy job," or unspecifically and undefinedly, "You've got to do better." And there is nothing which so quickly and completely destroys communications, rapport, mutuality — and builds antagonism and hostility. The reasons are that by *not* being defined and explicit, such comments imply necessary improvements in a man's basic character, as well as his performance; and by not focusing specifically on certain needs for improvement, they imply a need for improvement in *all* aspects and areas — a prospect which the worker necessarily regards as insurmountable and impossible, and therefore disheartening and demoralizing.

This lethally destructive force a supervisor attains by being negative should emphasize equally the opposite boundless and wonderfully beneficial impact he can attain by approaching personnel development positively. A supervisor's sensitiveness, thoughtfulness, constructiveness, comprehensiveness, and dispassionate perspective are the things which mark him to his workers as a positive leader.

Except for that rare individual who is so supremely egotistical that he lives exclusively by his own self-estimates and self-measurements, all men and women are beset by misgivings, critical and disparaging self-estimates, intimate feelings of lack of strength or capacity, questions of self-worth and self-value, overestimates of the courage and capacity of others. Depending on whether he is negative, caustic, pessimistic and obliquely critical, or is positive, sensitive, opportune, and constructive, a supervisor pours acid or balm on these human sensitivities and questions: negatively, he can do much to depreciate people; positively, he can help immeasurably to make them more confident, optimistic — *and productive.*

I frequently remember an 18-year-old volunteer seaman who came to my stateroom one day during World War II, requesting a chance to talk with me privately. At first, he refused to sit down, but stood self-consciously for a few moments before he blurted out, "Sir, I'm a bad sailor!" When I asked *why,* he said, "Because I'm afraid — I'm scared." I got up, crossed the stateroom, held out my hand and said, "Shake on it — you're one of the bunch! I'm scared, too. Everyone is scared — that's being human and being normal. If you *weren't* scared, you'd be a poor sailor — because you wouldn't be sensitive to dangers and responsive to the need for self-preservation."

The relieved look on his face was something I will never forget. Like most people, he had discovered a human characteristic within himself which, since he did not see it in other people, he regarded self-consciously as a frailty, a weakness, something despicable. But when he understood the basic humanness of his misgivings, he secured a sense of mutuality and companionship from the very same characteristics which had previously made him feel separated, alone, inferior. A great deal of my life — both personally and professionally — has been involved with assisting people to recognize the extent to which they should have well-justified self-confidence and optimism. And actually, this is nothing more than the realization that fears, misgivings, and critical self-judgment, which ordinarily we hide effectively, are common to all people, and most people's potentialities invariably far exceed their estimates and preconceived ideas of themselves.

Encouraging and Guiding Workers' Self-Development

Fortified with a comprehensive and thoughtful analysis, and with sensitivity and a constructive attitude, you are ready to bring out and develop the latent potentialities of your people — the people potential of yourself and of your job. Your people will rapidly recognize your positive and constructive time — and will respond in similar terms. Actually, if the session is properly handled, the worker will not regard it as critical and negative; instead, he will find it an effort on your part to reduce his general misgivings into diminished and specific realities — to put his improvement needs on a constructive, clear and surmountable basis — which he can attain.

The first step in such a planning session is to commend the worker for the five things which he does best and most effectively. This demonstrates to your employee that his work and efforts are being seen totally, comprehensively, constructively. It encourages him, and it reinforces him by giving him both a sense of attainment and a model for the attainment which he will be able to additionally secure through the improvement efforts and training which you next recommend.

In a sense, this is goal setting — with goals carefully delineated and deliberated, and selected as being those which are most pertinent and urgent. But you should be prepared in advance to discuss these things:

1. What the goals consist of.
2. Why they were selected.
3. What specifically is recommended to achieve these goals.
4. The type, nature, and elapsed-time requirement of any training which is suggested.
5. What follow-up and action are proposed upon completion of the training and development program.
6. What follow-up and discussion are planned during the interval taken by specifically recommended courses or studies.
7. What private availability for discussion and question the supervisor offers during the period of the training program.
8. What plans and schedules there are for additional comprehensive reviews of the worker's progress, attainment, and remaining development needs.

Training and development cannot be crammed down the throats of subordinates. And in fact, training and development lose many of the precious by-products of employee initiative, stimulation, interaction, participation, involvement, and exhilaration when they appear as a mandate, rigidly fixed, overly structured or generalized. Sensitively handled and flexibly administered, training and development plans and programs not only accomplish their own objectives more fully and satisfactorily, but, additionally, give progressive impulse to further and future participation, learning, and development by the worker.

Positive Tone Must Be Maintained

It is therefore vital that from the very initiation of interviews and discussions you should take great pains to assure the participation of the worker in the formulation of his own training and development programs. On the one hand, you should be well-prepared in advance to suggest specific methods, programs, and courses for the employee's development. But, on the other, you must treat these wisely and flexibly — do not present them as rigid requirements and fixed mandates. You should carefully involve and consider any and all alternatives which the worker may suggest.

Sometimes you will find that the alternative suggested by the employee may be more precisely suited to his needs and capacities — may actually be preferable, or may require a great deal more dedication on his part than you had anticipated you could expect from him.

From time to time supervisors find that their analysis of workers' training and development needs should be amended and adjusted. For example, there may be extenuating circumstances for present problems or inadequacies. Or some temporary current factors about which the supervisor did not know in the life of the worker may have momentarily distorted the picture of his most pressing training and development needs.

If you handle it in this manner, training and development interviews become truly mutual interest and mutual effort planning sessions. Sessions become more fun, more human, more relaxed, more productive. They accomplish their intended purpose to a degree which cannot be attained through any other approach. Additionally, they do the following:

1. Encourage the worker as to the prospect of his remedying of his problems.
2. Assure the ambitious worker of the prospect of growth, progress, and advancement.
3. Build workers' self-confidence and dedication.

4. Reflect to the worker that his work improvement and progress is an interest mutually shared by his supervisor.
5. Build communications ease and rapport between supervisors and subordinates.
6. Demonstrate the constructive, positive, equitable and helpful attitude of the supervisor; improve relationships and enhance loyalty and worker responsiveness.
7. Enable a supervisor to know and understand his people more comprehensively and sensitively.
8. Reassure the soundness, appropriateness, effectiveness, and workability of training and development plans and programs.
9. Provide the supervisor with keener and more dependable insight into the current and potential capacities of his work force.
10. Audit the gradual changes in potential or pending alterations in job content, work approaches, and occupational skill requirements of the department.

Discovering and Clarifying the Worker's "Talent Foundation"

You will find that the technique of highlighting the five "best" areas of the individual's accomplishment is highly effective in encouraging workers and demonstrating the comprehensiveness, consistency, and perspective of your reviews of their performance.

They help in another vital way, as well. Selected carefully from a comprehensive review of *all* the worker's performance areas, these five points very validly reflect the specific nature of his highest degree of capability and interest. Just as the "poorest" items signal the need and appropriateness of remedy, training and development, these "commended" areas indicate specific and suitable subjects and skills for further refinement and development, capitalization, intensification. They are things upon which to build positively and constructively; they are, in effect, the "talent foundation" of the worker.

Prior to any positive and dependable building efforts, there should be complete and encompassing understanding. Therefore, in addition to commending the employee for his performance in these subject areas, the supervisor should examine these factors:

1. Whether these are new or established areas of the worker's commendable performance;
2. What specific and useful training, education, or experience the worker may have had in these work-aspects;

3. How these items coincide with previous work and educational choices of the worker;

4. To what extent these assets were influenced by early interests or the occupational or non-vocational activities of the worker's parents and family;

5. The degree to which the worker has retained interest in the prospect and future of developing these particular talents; and

6. The extent to which these talents may be minimized or intensified by the worker's self-image and his concept of how the future prospects and potentialities of these talents support or diminish the possibility of attaining and fulfilling that self-image.

It may well be that the entire range and meaning of an employee's talent foundation will not be clearly revealed by the five items of most commendable performance. But these items will reveal enough so that a supervisory manager can explore and clarify them through interviews in which he utilizes these factors as preliminary guidelines.

Another helpful or supplementary means for you to use in discovering the needed initial information on a worker's talent foundation is psychological tests. Ordinarily, aptitude tests are used for this purpose, but I have found that interest tests serve my requirements favorably and satisfactorily. Talent and interest, after all, are closely and inseparably linked together. In viewing an employee's pattern of positive interests, and how these differentiate from negative interests, a great deal of insight can be gained into the individual's actual or latent talents.

It will often be found that the talent foundation of an individual may have remained undeveloped or underdeveloped, or may have been actually suppressed. This may have occurred because family, friends, or the individual himself did not visualize a very promising or attractive future in the development and utilization of his talent foundation. Or it may not have concurred with an individual's aspirations or self-image. In some cases, it may be because the talent foundation was never comprehensively understood, clarified, or related to occupational activities.

Psychological tests of interest patterns have the great advantage of clarity and perspective: and, unlike *activities* relating to an individual's talent foundation, pertinent interest cannot be suppressed or altered. However, these same guidelines can be developed through interviewing — if a supervisor is sensitive enough, and has the patience and deliberateness to seek to understand the individual's talent foundation comprehensively and well. It merely requires that he know what he is looking for — and that he protract and repeat interviews until he is fully sure that he has obtained all the necessary information, and that he has done so accurately.

Strengthening and Utilizing
the Employee's Talent Foundation

Ian Campbell, a roads construction worker, did a good basic job in the work which he was assigned, and often made thoughtful and useful suggestions on work method, approach, scheduling. His supervisor, Harry Becknell, thought that Ian had a lot to offer — could "go places" — and frequently told Ian so, in the specific terms of the talent foundation Ian had demonstrated and contributed. Because, as Harry noted, Ian's talents were not only in the technicalities of the job and his willingness to work, but also were in leadership, Harry particularly wanted Ian to prepare for supervisory assignment.

The constant changes and problems arising in work raised many questions on the part of other workers. They seemed to turn spontaneously to Ian, and he quickly and unhesitatingly provided useful, productive answers. But each time Harry tried to put Ian in charge of a work crew, Ian either refused, or did a poor job at it. Tests revealed that Ian was seriously — yet unjustifiably — lacking in self-confidence. His development program consisted of placing Ian in a supervisory position in which he felt that he had Harry's continuous support, and thus relied on his confidence in Harry, rather than on his own self-confidence. Over a period of time, Ian began to secure his sense of confidence from the work and results themselves, rather than from Harry's back-up; and he soon was fully and independently utilizing his talent foundation in effective and sensitive leadership.

Once you have discovered, clarified, and delineated a worker's talent foundation, it can be built on either directly or indirectly. If it appears, for example, that it is something which does not fit with his self-image or aspirations, you will find some fairly obvious and necessary corrective measures and actions by exploring these questions:

1. To what degree is the employee's talent foundation clear to him — and to what extent does he understand its meaning and ramifications?
2. Is the job or work for which the employee's talent foundation

would especially suit him, one whose content, status, or potentiality he underestimates?

3. Is the promotion possibility and ultimate assignment of his specific talent one with which he is unfamiliar, or which he minimizes?

4. Has the worker realistically faced the fact that his relative success and progress in fields outside his talent foundation will be substantially less, and more difficult to attain?

5. Does the worker have a sufficiently broad concept of the number and variety of occupations in which his talent foundation can be usefully and profitably identified?

6. What reasonable, suitable, and attractive alternative or additional prospects, possibilities about which he currently knows, can be explained and made attainable to him?

7. To what extent can some phase or aspect of his talent foundation be applied and developed in his current work and assignment?

8. To what extent are his hesitancies or inhibitions about his talent foundation due to unjustified or remediable questions about his confidence or capability in activities or knowledge fields which are required to support it?

9. To what degree has the worker faced previous occupational problems through misinterpretation or misapplication of his talent foundation?

Earlier in the book we mentioned the experiences of Steve Hunter, whose basic interest and talent foundation was responsive service to people. Steve had misjudged this, and had inappropriately allied himself with people "causes," rather than people themselves, and had gotten into difficulty. Next, he involved himself in people's "rights" — and that was nearly a personal catastrophe for him. His next effort was to be in food sales in underprivileged neighborhoods, which most certainly would have been a fiasco ending in bankruptcy. But fortunately, a wise supervisor recognized the real meaning and appropriate use of Steve's talent foundation — and guided him into training which gave full and constructive use and expression to Steve's unusual capacities.

As this suggests, there are two imperatives with respect to a worker's talent foundation. First, it must be seen and understood clearly and comprehensively. Second, it must be developed and built on accurately, appropriately, and objectively. In a sense, as a supervisory manager you must be an innovator and an opportunist *with* people and *for* people in the conduct of your job and the fulfillment of your responsibilities. You must have keen awareness of the job to be done — and the capacity to translate this into the employee's understanding, responsiveness, and effort, which get the job done. But perhaps to an even greater extent, you must be able to sensitively assess the capacities and talents of people, to visualize how these can be verified, developed, applied, and utilized — in future work, as well as in current activity.

Using Talent Foundation as a Basis of Motivation

Although employee motivations encompass a wide range of areas and impulses that are not directly reflected in vocational interest patterns, interests are a fundamental ingredient for motivation. For instance, fulfillment of the employee motivation toward a sense of belonging may depend heavily on companionship of interest if this is to be the nature of the relationship. Motivation toward security also ties in closely with interest areas in which a worker can develop a sense of self-worth and well-being. And it is possible also to determine the extent to which interests and personality traits mutually support each other, and thereby potentially contribute to a worker's sense of well-being and self-worth.

To illustrate, it is obvious that a person who was intensely interested in sales and selling but who was basically shy, reticent, and introverted, would find no personality-trait support for his interests; but the same interest pattern in a person who was outgoing, sociable, and somewhat extroverted would find his personality, nature, and interest all in coinciding focus. This suggests that he could potentially do well in the fields of his interests, and would derive a sense of well-being, self-worth, and accomplishment from such activities.

To a large extent, talent foundation synthesizes these several factors which individually influence worker motivation. Because talent foundation suggests a combination of interests, aptitude, and personality, it ties more clearly and comprehensively to employee motivation. Also, talent foundation reflects a worker's area of greatest potentiality. Thus, to the extent that the talent foundation is adequately guided, oriented, and developed, it is the greatest potential source for fulfillment of the motivations of self-worth, sense of belonging, security, and progress.

Speaking in a negative sense, we know that a worker cannot attain a total sense of self-worth and fulfillment until all of his strongly positive interests are activated and exercised; if it is not possible to identify and utilize all positive interests in an occupation, the worker must assure that his vocational, avocational, and recreational activities somehow combine to encompass these interests. Similarly, failure to fully identify, exercise, and utilize the total talent foundation substantially reduces the prospect of a worker's motivational fulfillment and satisfaction.

Without question, an employee's talent foundation represents the sphere in which he can be most effective and successful, and in which he can find his fullest measure of motivational fulfillment. Your paramount problem as a supervisor, therefore, is to discover the talent foundation, understand it, and identify its prospects in ways which attract the worker and which stimulate his effort and support in its fullest development.

11

MAKING GROUP DEVELOPMENT PROGRAMS FIT YOUR PEOPLE POTENTIAL

"This training program irritates me," a worker declared to Vic Hanson, his supervisor. "If it were not basically a good program — or if its material weren't along the lines of my needs and interests — it would have bored me. But the agenda of the program is really good; the trouble is that you've got too much of a mix of levels and degrees of knowledge and interest. It really gets me ruffled when one guy has to go over some minor or elementary point again and again and again in order to understand it, or some other guy tries to rush through some essential part merely because he is not interested."

When Individual or Group Plans Fit Best

This identical problem has considerably influenced the educational industry in its development of various forms of "individualized instruction." People vary considerably in their speed of learning and assimilation, and sometimes in the form which instruction should take. Purely generalized programs which must serve groups which have not been pre-selected for their similarity necessarily are geared to the average speed, pace, and content. The result is that fast learners become bored or irritated, and slow learners become upset and confused. Only those few whose needs in pace and content happen to coincide with the somewhat arbitarily and theoretically drawn "average" find the program fully stimulating, challenging, and helpful.

Actually, the need for individualized instruction is even greater in industry than it is in education: the background, experience, training, and development of industrial workers vary far more widely than the earlier development of young children of fairly equal ages. Thus, in addition to the need for providing for differences in pace of learning, there is intense need in industry to provide also for vast variables in prior education, training, and development.

To be effective, learning must do more than provide knowledge and information in which a worker is deficient; training must also be planned and prepared in a format, manner, sequence, pace, timing, and degree of detail suited to the worker's interests and capacities of assimilation. In effect, training must be *prescribed* on the basis of a worker's knowledge *deficiencies,* but must be *based* on a worker's *capacities.* It requires intensive study and understanding of the individual worker.

Individualizing Your Training Program

Particularly in general training programs which include a variety of specific craft and skill areas, it is sometimes useful to divide the material into units or segments. For example, if the total program is to include sections on mathematics, blueprint reading, the use of transits, barometers and gauges, or similar units, the relative amount of previous experience or training which individual workers have had in each of these spheres can be readily determined from a review of personnel records and discussions with the employee.

When it is found that a worker has had recent training or experience with the subject, it is usually best to let him completely omit that particular phase of the program. If a worker has had adequate training and experience in the subject area, but considerable time has elapsed since he was actually involved in it, the final portion of the training program for that subject can be used as a refresher as it is simultaneously being used as a summary for those who have been currently participating. However, while a training program is in process, there should be a continuity of involvement for *all* participants. So when some are not scheduled into all of the sessions because of prior experience and training, appropriate alternative courses or self-development studies of approximately the same time requirements should be substituted.

Suitable individual programs are somewhat more difficult to develop for workers whose learning speed or prior training and experience are less than that of the "average" for whom the general course structure was designed. When there is only minor disparity between a worker's training or speed of learning and that of the rest of the group, it is sometimes possible to use a tutoring system: such participants attend regular sessions, but reserve their questions and requests for supplementary individual "help sessions." Otherwise, it becomes necessary to provide entirely separate and longer courses on either an in-company basis, or through local educational programs and resources.

Individualizing Your Worker Development

"Every worker is a little different — and I feel that each worker's differences in interest, learning, speed, capacity, hopes and aims, all must be known individually and treated differently," suggested one foreman. "You've got to do it this way to be accurate, and to develop a program which really fits a guy and helps him. Furthermore, you find that as you handle it in this way you get to know each worker a little bit better, and that he responds better and more constructively to training and development. By planning it and discussing it individually with each worker, you make him know *why* and *how* it would help him — and he feels better about the program, and he feels better about you."

He went on to suggest that many training programs are too specific in their purpose — are adopted to assist or remedy one specific thing. In his belief it is far preferable to try to define an individual's total needs in education and development, and then to establish a comprehensive broad program of development for each individual worker. Then, he feels, it is relatively easy to determine what training is needed, and where and how it should be provided.

Often, a worker's paramount and most immediate needs are in the development of work habits, work concepts, and work relationships. When these needs are satisfied, the worker approaches training with a greater recognition of its pertinence, and thus with greater interest and enthusiasm.

Experience with one program of training for "underprivileged minorities" provides an extreme but clear illustration of the high-impact value of such advance study, preparation, and planning. Mostly young, the majority of the trainees had never previously worked. Work habits had never been developed and disciplined. Embarrassed in their lack of even elementary know-how, they were hesitant to ask questions, and thereby became apathetic and unresponsive. Most felt that they were placed and protected by government edict — and lived on a day-to-day basis of income, with no concern or aspiration about future prospects.

"As a result of this, most were virtually unable to relate to each other, and to other workers," the foreman explained. "And when they found out that work is team effort, that it helped them to relate to others and to have an identity with and among other people, it seemed to really motivate them and bring them to life. Motivation is a funny thing — it feeds and rejuvenates itself. Once these guys found out that they could get relationship and identity through work, they wanted to learn more, and became very devoted to training, learning, and development."

An added note of caution: don't set goals too high, because you will discourage your workers with "an insurmountable task"; but make the goals sufficiently ambitious to keep them from being exceeded. Goals which are exceeded tend to bring on a "fat cat" attitude. As one training director suggested, "People have got to be stretched a bit — and feel that they're being stretched. Then they start to recognize that their potentialities exceed their initial self-measurement."

Placing Individuals into Group Programs

Group training can be a very useful medium for teaching and guiding workers into productive interaction and team effort. But it cannot be an abstract and generalized assignment. It must be prefaced by individual review, and it must be a consistent and compatible phase of a comprehensive and clearly communicated program of worker education and development. Specifically, for maximum results, as a supervisor-manager you must:

1. Study personnel records, background information pertaining to experience and education.
2. Clarify the details and particulars of the worker's background through discussion and questions.
3. Determine the worker's major interests, aspirations, goals, attitudes, and values.
4. Ascertain the appropriateness of the worker's interests and aspirations in terms of his current and potential knowledge and development.
5. Calculate the margin of difference between the worker's aspirations and his current know-how and development.
6. Enumerate the sources and resources through which the specifically needed development can be attained.
7. Sequence the items of development in terms of their interrelationship and dependency on each other — and individual preparedness needed as a preface to group participation.

8. Select the resources which are best suited to the worker, his schedules, his availability, his capacity to assimilate.
9. Analyze, from a specification outline of current and prospective occupational responsibilities, the elements in which the worker does best, does most poorly, and in which he is in most urgent need for immediate development.
10. Observe the relationship and interaction which the worker has developed with other people in the department.
11. Confer with the worker, suggest your tentative outline as a guideline, and secure his participation in formulating and finalizing his educational development program.
12. Indicate the specific values and progress which will be assured by dedication to the program and successful completion of its requirements.
13. Follow up at frequent intervals — and be sure that the worker is aware of your continuing interest and accessibility.

The final advice in this list is placed as number thirteen as a reminder that your program will be an unlucky one if this item is neglected or forgotten.

Easy and Accurate Ways of Setting Up Department Programs

Many supervisory managers and most companies fail to recognize the inseparable relationship between analysis of training needs and appraisal of worker performance. The highlighting and clarification of worker needs in training and development is one of several extremely valuable by-products of employee appraisal — and comprehensive appraisal of the individual employee's performance is the most accurate and dependable assessment of worker training, education, and development that can be obtained by any means.

Earlier in this volume we talked about what employee appraisal instruments and programs should consist of, how appraisal should be conducted in order to be dependable and effective, and in order to achieve its vital role in assessing, activating, and insuring your people potential. In that section, we referred to methods of using comprehensive review of worker qualifications, responses, performance, and work attitudes to highlight the individual's most valuable contribution, and his most urgent need for remedy and development.

To do an accurate, fair, and objective job of discovering the major strengths and weaknesses of a worker's performance, you should consider carefully how he fulfills each and every detail of the work and work-related activity to which he is assigned. It is only through the summation of such detailed individual appraisals that the total training and development needs of your department or unit as a whole can be analyzed accurately, dependably, and inclusively.

Construction superintendent Bill Hatch expressed it, "Any department or working unit is a team or a chain of human reaction and interaction; and any chain is as good and as strong as its weakest link. Pace, productivity, and flexibility are governed by your poorest or weakest worker, not by your best and strongest." In any and all things, any unit or department must be seen as an aggregate or sum total of the individuals it contains.

Assuring Appropriateness of Your Programs

A simple but comprehensive list of all the things you expect and require of your workers — qualification, skills, attitudes, responses, flexibility, interaction — provides an excellent checklist for determining and analyzing a worker's individual performance and his training and development needs. Job descriptions are helpful in the initial steps of composing such a list, but job descriptions and specifications consist primarily of qualifications and activities lists: thus, the performance-development list must be enlarged to include items of conduct, attitude, response, work habits, interaction, improvement efforts, and the like. In final form, the performance-development list will usually contain 50 to 75 items.

Suppose, for instance, that your performance-development list consists of 60 items. As noted earlier, as you use this in review of a worker, you will select five items which reflect what the worker does best, and five in which he most needs improvement and development. The latter five items are the most accurate and dependable highlighting you can get of an employee's needs in training, education, development, and improvement — especially when this list has been reviewed and discussed in detail with the worker.

Now you have an accurate and dependable ingredient for an accurate and dependable analysis of total or aggregate training and development needs of your department as a whole. To utilize it:

1. Scan the individual performance reviews of each worker in the department.
2. Record the items or their numbers which you have marked as each worker's five most important and pressing needs for improvement and development.

You may well find, for instance, that you have indicated that 50 or 60 percent of your workers need training and development in one particular item. This immediately suggests to you the specific enrollment of any pertinent program you may formulate and adopt. In the range of items you have highlighted in the individual reports, you have defined the range and scope of your most suitable departmental program of training and development. If you find that you have indicated that 75 percent or more of your workers need training and development in, say, three identical items, this is a special signal to you. It may be that your department is newly staffed: if it is not, you should seriously consider whether your individual appraisals have been conducted accurately and fairly or whether or not you have been deficient in the training, development, and leadership you have been providing your people.

A Note of Warning

Remember, as suggested several times, *do not compare* your workers one with another, except in matters of rewards which are to be selected and awarded on the basis of relative performance or contribution. You may wish to utilize the specific capabilities of one of your best-performing workers as a beginning general guideline in what a performance standard should be, and ideas regarding the extent and ingredients of training by which this level of skill and performance can be developed. But do not use the worker himself as a standard. Analyze in detail what it is in the volume, quality, and nature of this worker's performance which makes you regard it as a suitable and acceptable standard; then depersonalize the standard by adding to it considerations other than those of the worker whose work activity you have utilized as an initial guideline in setting up the performance standard. Best of all, look over your entire work crew, see "who does what best" in various aspects of the total work activity of the department; then put these together in an impersonal composite of the work and performance standards of the department.

Every long-experienced supervisor has ultimately discovered that utilizing any one worker as a standard (or, as some have sarcastically termed it, a "paragon of performance") creates several serious problems:

1. It does not adequately clarify and define what the standard implies or consists of.

2. It reflects a personal consideration and response which implies favoritism and inequitableness.
3. It does not clarify the limitations — where the personal example starts and stops — and thereby unintentionally but importantly introduces *other* factors of the individual worker's performance and relationships which seriously impair the standard, and other workers' reaction to it.
4. It discourages and antagonizes other workers — and, because of its personal connotation, makes progress and ultimate attainment an insurmountable task.
5. It creates disharmony, jealousy, friction, and unhealthy competitiveness and interaction between employees.
6. It isn't accurate — and it doesn't work.

Judging Training Theories by Your Own Practical Experience

By itself, the need for individualization of workers' programs of education and development reflects that training plans and programs cannot be selected arbitrarily or on the basis of generalized conclusions. The more precisely training is matched to the specific needs and capacities of the individual worker, the more effective it becomes; and the more training is planned as a consistent part of the total broad development of the individual worker, the more its value is increased through his resulting motivation and progressive skills and capacities. At best, so-called "canned" or arbitrary approaches in programs fail to fulfill training objectives; at worst, they cause resentment and negative reaction among employees.

But training concepts and theories must themselves be critically examined before they are adopted. After all, they must fit the specific requirements, needs, natures, and capacities of the individual workers for whom they are being considered. And the appropriate approaches, as well as the content, of training depend upon the characteristics which you have carefully examined in your analysis and planning: worker's background, qualifications, capacities, sensitivities, attitudes, responses, current stage of development, future needs.

There are a number of newly popular theories, techniques, and approaches in training: for example, group dynamics, sensitivity training, confrontation sessions, and a variety of others. Each of these has basic substance, purpose, and value. There is no reason to debate their relative values or effectiveness, because all that you really need to determine is how appropriate they are for your own work force and the training needs and problems you are attempting to resolve.

Much of the criticism you read about these techniques and theories pertains to *how* they are used and when and with whom they are applied, rather than to the soundness of the general theories themselves. In many instances, they have been applied by people who were technically competent in the workings of the theories, but were not sensitively and adequately grounded in an understanding of people. Sound usage demands that both knowledge of people and knowledge of technique be carefully and sensitively blended. This is why it is my strong belief that successful use of such devices demands careful review by people who sensitively know people — in other words, by supervisor-managers. Only they have the day-to-day observation and experience with workers which provides the sensitive knowledge and understanding of people essential in determining the suitability, soundness, practicality, and humanness of any plan or program designed to influence people.

To illustrate the way in which some programs have cast negative shadows on potentially worthwhile techniques, a staff group for a New England university prepared a "confrontation seminar" which all supervisory personnel from one company were required to attend. To reinforce the impact of the seminar, it was announced that this was a test — and that any person who did not attend the entire seminar would lose his supervisory position. More than 50 percent of the group left before the end of the seminar — and several of them never returned to their company.

Designers of the program had carried the "confrontation" to such extremes that they had used hidden cameras and tape recorders wherever the audience members were expected to go at any time during the seminar — even in the bedrooms and lavatories. Participants were later subjected to simultaneous playback of four individual recordings, as accompanying pictures were projected on four huge screens in the lecture hall. I talked with eight supervisors who had attended the seminar. One of them remarked, "It's been only six months since the episode. So perhaps it isn't fair to say that I'll never get over it — but I honestly don't think that I will!"

But from the standpoint of more modulated and sensible applications of these new theories and techniques, let's examine one which has worked effectively in some situations and see what aspect of your experience helps you to judge its possible appropriateness for your own work group. In one form of group dynamics, workers are picked at random and put together, without prior explanation or

guidance, in a soundproofed room in which there are no such attention diverters as windows, pictures, or decorations. Emphasis is
placed on the fact that selection is random — people are intentionally not "homogeneous" in background, position, development, interest, or verbal ability. Silence is the extreme stimulus — because
without an established purpose or explanation, each person is stark-
ly and nakedly individual, without any initial sense of relationship
to the other participants.

You know, from your own experience and observation, that —

1. Your work group is comprised of verbal and non-verbal people in
   approximately a 40-to-60 ratio.
2. Among your less-verbal workers are some people who have extreme difficulty in communicating and relating — and who are
   extremely sensitive, hypertense, and filled with feelings of inferiority because of it.
3. All of your people fundamentally and vitally need interrelationships with other people — and among your non-verbal people, this
   is not only more of a problem, but is a more extreme sensitivity.
4. The beginning need and development of most of your workers
   centers in knowledge deficiencies — and as that need is met and
   fulfilled, self-confidence is increased, and hypersensitivity is
   diminished.

In other words, your knowledge and understanding of your people
tells you whether or not — or when and how — a training device
can be adopted and applied appropriately and helpfully.

Does this suggest, for instance, that such things as group dynamics
or sensitivity training should not be used at all? No; instead, as a
matter of fact, it reflects that such devices can be immensely helpful (a) when they are introduced at the appropriate time, stage, and
sequence in the development program of the individual worker;
(b) when the specific methods, aspects, and agenda of the program
are suited to the responses, as well as to the needs and capacities of
the individuals involved; and (c) when adequate consideration has
been devoted to the effect of a technique on the workers' capacities,
as well as their deficiencies.

Consider, for a moment, a quite homogeneous group of workers
— men and women who initially were lacking in self-confidence,
relatively low in skills, somewhat restricted in verbal abilities — who
have very successfully completed several phases of development
of important skills and capacities. At this stage of their development there is need to reinforce their self-confidence, and provide

them with an added awareness of the importance of their newly developed skills and their competence in this field. A "think-tank" type of group interaction, which pertains largely to matters relating to the skills and knowledge in which they have strongly and competently developed, can help immensely.

Adding Meaning and Stimulation to Training Programs

"To give real stimulation to training and development, you must provide something significant and meaningful to symbolize the worker's successful efforts and achievements in the program," a foreman suggested. Behavioral scientists and motivational specialists also suggest incorporating "reward" stimulation in any efforts to motivate people. If workers are being trained toward a specific occupation or occupational classification, such assignment should immediately follow successful completion of the training program. Occasionally, when full promotion steps are not available or possible, some wage adjustments can be made. But it reduces the long-range effectiveness of any program when the goals and the implied promises of the training are not awarded soon after the completion of the training requirements.

Motivation equally means to take care not to *demotivate*. So remember, too, that training can be either a stimulation or a stigma. If the program is not properly dignified and given stature, it may have the effect described by one worker: "It makes me feel as if I'm 'different' — not quite a full-fledged employee." Similarly, a supervisor suggested that apprenticeship training for "underprivileged minorities" makes participants carry the classifications of "underprivileged" and "minorities" at all times and in all situations if such programs are not integrated with other training activity, and unless trainees to whom these classifications do not apply are interspersed among them in more than "token" numbers. I have seen such "minority" classification in training have an adverse effect even when the ethnic group which the trainees represented was an actual *majori y* group in a company's local plant employment.

To return to he question of rewards on completion of training, "a buck in the pocket" is never an ample substitute for "a pat on the back." Both should be built into a training program in order to make it fully stimulating and rewarding. You are very well aware of the effect your own attitudes and values have upon the reactions and responses of your people. If you have been painstakingly accurate in selecting and assigning training, you have led your workers to feel that the program is suitable and appropriate. If you thereafter reflect interest and enthusiasm for the program and for a worker's efforts and activities in it, you will immeasurably enhance and increase his valuation of the program — and his interest and responsiveness to the training it includes. The frosting on the cake is the opportunity this provides you for sincerely demonstrating the thoughtfulness and suitability of your recommendations and guidance, and your interest in the worker and his development — a group of pluses, each of which adds tremendously to your people potential, and your attainment of it.

In summary, there are six ways in which you can add vitality, stimulation, and effectiveness to even the most carefully selected program of worker development:

1. Be interested: miss no opportunity for reminding each participating worker of the value, stature, and potentialities of training.
2. Follow up: establish specific routine periods for conferences with individual trainees, commending progress and discussing their comments and questions.
3. Maintain communications: in addition to the established routines of follow up, take every opportunity for casual comment — and also, to reassure the workers of your availability for discussion, comment, and questions.
4. Select "bench-marks": particularly in long or diverse programs of training and development, be sure that there are clear stages of development to which a trainee can look forward during the program, and at which he can feel some specific sense of progress and achievement.
5. Make it important: reflect your interest in the effects of the program; repeatedly identify its value to the worker; indicate your interest in the worker.
6. Provide rewards: completion certificates help; promotion, transfers, or re-assignments in terms of newly attained skill levels help; but whatever else is offered, personal congratulation and commendation are vital.

Your progress reviews are actually motivation sessions, when they are properly and sensitively handled. You transform a worker's needs and developments from deficiencies into unrealized potentialities which can be attained through training, effort, and commitment. In this light, progress reviews are not fault-finding sessions;

they are mutual-interest conferences on worker progress and development. They are, in reality, the door-opener to your full attainment of your people potential.

BIBLIOGRAPHY

Bagrit, Sir Leon. *Automation.* Mentor Books.

Barrett, Jon H. *Individual Goals and Organization Objectives.* University of Michigan.

Carnegie, Dale. *How to Win Friends and Influence People.*

Carter, Michael. *Into Work.*

Combs, Avila, Purkey. *Basic Concepts for the Helping Professions.* Allyn & Bacon Pub.

DeMente, Boyer. *Japanese Manners and Etiquette in Business.* East Asia Publishing.

Durant, William James. *The Story of Civilization.* Simon & Schuster.

Foulsham, W., & Co., LTD. *Managing Your Manpower.*

Hoffer, Eric. *The Ordeal of Change.* Harper & Row.

Howe, Reuel L. *Survival Plus.* Seabury Press.

Humble, J. W. *Improving Management Performance.* Management Publications, Ltd.

King, David. *Training Within the Organization.* Tavistock Publications.

King-Scott, P. *Industrial Supervision.* Pitman Press.

Koch, Adrienne. *Philosophy for a Time of Crisis.*

Levenstein, Aaron. *Why People Work.* Collier Books.

Lewis, Edwin. *Developing Women's Potential.* University of Iowa Press.

MacHorton, Ian. *How to Get a Better Job in Management.* Mercury House.

Menninger, Karl. *The Human Mind.* Literary Guild.

Mumford, Alan. *The Manager and Training.* Pitman Publishing.

Packard, Vance. *The Pyramid Climbers.* Mc-Graw-Hill.

Paul, W.J., and K.B. Robertson. *Job Enrichment and Employee Motivation.* Gower Press.

Peale, Norman Vincent. *The Power of Positive Thinking.* Prentice-Hall.

Peter, Lawrence J., and Raymond Hull. *The Peter Principle.* Bantam Books.

Roe, Anne. *The Psychology of Occupations.* John Wiley & Sons.

Silberman, Charles. *Crisis in the Classroom.* Random House, 1970.

Taylor, Linda King. *Not By Bread Alone.* Business Books, Ltd., London.

Toffler, Alvin. *Future Shock.* Random House, 1970.

VanLoon, Hendrick Willem. *The Story of Mankind.* Boni & Liveright.

Williams, M. R. *Supervisory Management in the Office.* Heinemann, London.